MW00827577

RAPID WEIGHT LOSS HYPNOSIS

Extreme Weight-Loss Hypnosis for Woman! How to Fat Burning & Calorie Blast, Lose Weight with Meditation & Affirmations, Mini Habits, Self-Hypnosis. Stop Emotional Eating!

By

Karen Loss

TABLE OF CONTENTS

COPYRIGHTS

©Copyright by Karen Loss 2020

All rights reserved

This book: "**RAPID WEIGHT LOSS HYPNOSIS:** Extreme Weight-Loss Hypnosis for Woman! How to Fat Burning & Calorie Blast, Lose Weight with Meditation & Affirmations, Mini Habits, Self-Hypnosis. Stop Emotional Eating!**"**

Written by Karen Loss

This document aims to provide precise and reliable details on this subject and the problem under discussion.

The product is marketed on the assumption that no officially approved bookkeeping or publishing house provides other available funds.

Where a legal or qualified guide is required, a person must have the right to participate in the field.

A statement of principle, which is a subcommittee of the American Bar Association, a committee of publishers and Associations and approved. A copy, reproduction, or distribution of parts of this text, in electronic or written form, is not permitted.

The recording of this Document is strictly prohibited, and any retention of this text is only with the written permission of the publisher and all Liberties authorized.

The information provided here is correct and reliable, as any lack of attention or other means resulting from the misuse or use of the procedures, procedures, or instructions contained therein is the total, and absolute obligation of the user addressed.

The author is not obliged, directly or indirectly, to assume civil or civil liability for any restoration, damage, or loss resulting from the data collected here. The respective authors retain all copyrights not kept by the publisher.

The information contained herein is solely and universally available for information purposes. The data is presented without a warranty or promise of any kind.

The trademarks used are without approval, and the patent is issued without the trademark owner's permission or protection. The logos and labels in this book are the property of the owners themselves and are not associated with this text.

CHAPTER 1: INTRODUCTION

There is no denying that obesity and the associated health problems are one of the biggest challenges faced not only by western countries but also in many other developing countries. The Journal of Health Economics provides more than $ 200 billion annually in the United States for medical obesity research costs. According to SAD (Standard

American Diet), processed foods and beverages high in fat, sodium, and sugar that are spread to other countries increase heart disease, diabetes, and other life-threatening problems. The food industry has been treating overweight people for decades (more than $ 2 billion in the U.S. alone in 2015) - most people have tried various diets and other programs that either fail or work temporarily and have made them even more discouraged.

You will find tons of help books that give you diet plans, but they are useless. If you question this, when trying to meet the diet's requirements, let alone allow all of the ingredients, you will lose weight with only the effort required to follow the diet. But here is the most critical statistic that anyone who wants to lose weight should know. Most people who lose weight successfully go on a diet and gain even more weight in the first year! These statistics include people who have participated in The Biggest Loser or whose stomachs have been stapled. This is the most suppressed statistic in the food industry: only 3 in 100 people who reach their goal manage to maintain this weight loss beyond the first year.

A post-mortem with the rest of the 97 people who struggled to keep their weight down showed that they were much hungry after trying their regular diet again than they were before the weight loss program. They have been busy eating since the end of their diet, and some are crazy about food.

From the perspective of human evolution, eating is the phenomenon of the last second. Historically telling, the 1920s was a mere failure to promote less eating, but as a society, the cycle of dietary habits that triggered famine brain mechanisms began until the late 1960s.

A weight-loss diet, by definition, requires a reduction in food intake below what the body needs to maintain its current form. There is no real food shortage, but all the built-in mechanisms that ensure our survival record fat loss. This reduction triggers a neural circuit that uses an army of hormones that cause the order of overeating. This mechanism is simply called the famine brain. Overeating works as the brain's primary reward system for dieting. Unfortunately, researchers have found that weight loss of all kinds uses our neurochemical weapons. If you have too much fat, your body won't know. It only "knows" if you risk losing fat. In a brave attempt to regain homeostasis, our system lowers the hormone levels that signal satiety (leptin and insulin) and pumps the fasting hormone 'ghrelin' into the bloodstream. This hormone results in heightened craving for food leading to extra calorie intake and eventually more weight gain.

Scientists are not yet aware of how the brain and physical starvation system interact to support or override each other. What we know is that many regular diets lead to a mind obsessed with food. Therefore, the root of the problem lies in the brain where this cycle continues.

The way we can save us from this cycle is to optimize brain activity. This optimization and control are what you will learn in this book. Thankfully, we can change our brain patterns to behave differently. In this book, we will study self-hypnosis, cognitive behavioral therapy, sleep learning system, and meditation to control our brain and overcome food cravings. To simply put, we will optimize the brain activity.

It also covers seemingly ordinary but very influential tricks to get rid of excess fat. We will also learn a few practical habits employing the techniques mentioned above. We will investigate the location of the problem and how it affects us so that we can suggest targeted actions.

CHAPTER 2: ROOT CAUSES OF FOOD ADDICTION

Until now, you have been listening to multiple reasons for weight gain. Some may say that overeating causes weight gain; some may believe that it is because of hormonal issues. Some may say that the lazy routine is the cause of obesity. We cannot deny them. All of them are correct. But if you dig deeper, you'll find causes of most problems in your head, including overeating and other causes that are mentioned.

How does a food addict's brain differ from a naturally lean female brain? This section describes the main characteristics of the differences in the mind, especially in food addicts.

We are crazy about food. -We usually force us to eat. -We need more food to be full. -We often suffer from hunger. -We respond more strongly to food references. -Emotional imbalance causes brain hunger in us.

Functional magnetic resonance imaging (fMRI) uses the magnetic properties of blood to determine which area of the brain is most active when a subject experience a particular event. Neuroscientists can measure brain activity when food addicts are exposed to food labels, eat delicious foods, or eat certain foods. "It's like training," explains Dr. Ashley

Gerhardt. "When you train a particular muscle, blood flows into that area. The brain seems to be working the same way, and you can track which area of the brain receives the most blood."

fMRI consistently shows that the convergence zone for sensory information is the prefrontal cortex, related to reward stimuli, particularly primary reinforcement factors such as food. To elucidate the neurobiological mechanisms by which weight, mood, and age affect the appetite response, Dr. Gerhardt presented healthy, average weight, obese adolescent and adult women with color photographs of foods with different fat content and caloric density while undergoing fMRI (high reward vs. low reward). She shows that food-addicted women responded to highly rewarded foods in the same way drug addicts respond to drugs.

Dr. Bart Hoebel, originally from Princeton University, he was one of the first to study a mouse for sugar addiction. He showed that every drop of sweet they swallowed increased the levels of dopamine. Similar to human addicts, Hoebel's rat sugar developed a hypersensitive dopamine receptor that was hyperresponsive to a variety of drugs, and its changes were long-lasting. Even after a month of self-discipline, the taste of sugar stimulates the rat to become addicted.

In a similar study, in Birmingham at the University of Alabama, Dr. Mary Boggiano figured out that a junk food attack in rats elicits the same pleasing receptors in the brain that drug addicts are stimulated when they ingest drugs. Dr. Boggiano's oleo-conjugated rats have long-term changes in endogenous opioids in the brain and become abnormally responsive to delicious food.

And if this cream puff tastes as good as sex, it's no coincidence. The dopamine reward system is the way we feel good and is associated with obsessive gambling, substance abuse, and sex. Food satisfaction results from some of the same neural signals and pathways that regulate orgasm. As a result, hundreds of neuroscientists have begun to record that obesity, eating disorders, and even healthy appetite resemble addiction. "Repeating dopamine over and over is what substance abuse does," says Dr. Hoebel. "This makes you wonder if food may have addictive properties.

Food gives you a discreet physiological response in the same way that drug consumption gives you a huge response," says psychiatrist Walter H. Kaye, director of the Eating Disorders Program at the University of California, San Diego. The drug takes over the food reward. "Drugs are addictive because they open the way for appetite.

Like other drug therapies, food therapy is an attempt to achieve the dopamine levels required by all addicts. In a 1954 study identifying amusement centers, two McGill University researchers, Dr. James Olds and Dr. Peter Milner, documented the effects of dopamine. In this study, rats were able to push the bar to electrically stimulate the amusement center or push the bar for food. Dr. Olds and Dr. Milner said electrical stimulation of rats to an amusement center is more rewarding than eating. The experience was so satisfying that the hungry rat ignored the food for pleasure the electrical impulse from the entertainment facility gave her. Some rats stimulated the brain more than 2,000 times an hour for 24 consecutive hours. Most mice died on an empty stomach.

Heroin and cocaine addicts also happen to forget about eating and lose a lot of weight while taking the drug. This fact explains why you get dopamine fixes from other sources. The first stage of love, all the activities that we find so enjoyable, we don't eat much and forget to eat! Poisoning is high dopamine, not food. If this mechanism fails, we end up eating too much food, obsessed with repairing dopamine.

So, that's how you overeat. You do not eat because you like it, but you eat because you are compelled to eat. Now we will look into types of overeating.

CHAPTER 3: TYPES OF OVEREATING

Based on the reason, the habit of overeating can be divided into two types:

- Obsessive overeating
- Compulsive overeating

OBSESSIVE OVEREATING

Dr. Gearhardt, a scholarship recipient at the Yale University Rudd Center for Food Policy and Obesity Center, conducted a neurobiological study and documented similarities in how the brain responds to drugs and delicious foods. Like drug addicts, food addicts struggle with increasing desires, encourage them to eat in response to food alerts, and may feel out of control when eating delicious food. Just as one drink sends an alcoholic beverage to a bend, some biscuits can also cause seizures.

"The results of this study back the theory that increasing expectations for food may partially cause forced diets," said Gearhardt. Depending on the expected food intake, participants with higher levels of food obsession showed more significant activity in the parts of the brain supposed to create the motivation and urge to eat, but with suppression of inhibiting mechanism during impulses. Responsible for consumption, which showed less activity in the area of responsibility.

Gene Jack Wang, MD, director of medicine at the Brookhaven National Laboratory in Upton, NY, and Dr. Nora Volkow, director of the 'National Institute on Drug Abuse,' said this was just a perspective on human imaging studies and grilled chicken. The smell of hamburgers and pizza releases dopamine into the brain. This food stimulus significantly increased dopamine levels in the minds of gluttons, but not in non-gluttons. The amount released correlates with the intensity of one's desire for food for a long time, the subjective impression "I seek for it."

"This is how our brain controls our desires," said Dr. Wang, many food addicts feel weak in their ability to control when and how much they eat. The entertainment center contains the striatum, a part of the limbic system that contributes to motivation, and the neurotransmitter dopamine, which controls the quest for pleasure and produces pleasure. "Now we're not just talking about balancing the energy level," he says. "We are discussing human psychology," said Wang.

COMPULSIVE OVEREATING

The ventral striatum of the brain is best known for its role in motor pathway planning and coordination. Still, it is also involved in a variety of other cognitive processes, including executive functions such as working memory. In humans, the striatum is activated by reward-related stimuli, but also by an aversive, novel, unexpected, or intense triggers and the symptoms associated with such events. When you see the brain like a train, the striatum on the ventral side is the accelerator.

When food enters the human body, it stimulates the amusement center, which increases the flow of dopamine. When overeating becomes standard behavior, three things happen:

1) The reward system is kidnapped,

2) Neuroplastic changes occur,

3) Serotonin and GABA (inhibitor) neurotransmitters involved in the "brake system" are reduced.

Food addiction confuses entertainment centers. It is more like when brakes of a train break down, and runaway trains eventually jump off the tracks. All are accelerators, no brakes. Forced or compulsive overeating is like this.

CHAPTER 4: WHY DO WE OVERHEAT?

Eating is one of our biological needs and is ensured by the joy we feel when we eat. But as soon as we got hooked on food, like long-term alcoholics became able to drink everyone under the table, and as drug addicts needed more and more medicine, we develop greater tolerance to food. All forms of addiction require increasingly addictive substances to reach dopamine levels.

Chronically strong drinkers have few signs of addiction, with high blood alcohol levels, which are either impossible or fatal to non-drinkers. Tolerance facilitates the consumption of overconsumption of alcohol, which leads to long term physical addiction. Similarly, the addict's brain needs more food to produce the amounts of dopamine that are associated with normal high-grade foods.

Men who rely on web pornography during the study are one of the most moving examples of forgiveness. As soon as a man completely relies on this form of dopamine fixation, he reports that he is unable to be agitated or satisfied during intercourse with a real woman. They take months to go without an X-rated website and endure severe withdrawal symptoms before they can regain the joy of interacting with a real woman.

In 2001, along with his colleagues Dr. Volkow, including Dr. Wang, a Ph.D., obtained brain scans of overweight and normal-weight volunteers to study the enumeration of dopamine receptors. Dr. Wang noticed that overweight people had lesser dopamine receptors-the the more obese they were, the fewer these important receptors they had (the brains of addicts). He says the brains of overweight people and drug addicts are strikingly similar: "Both have fewer dopamine receptors than normal subjects."

All addicts are looking for a solution, but if we become more resistant to our drugs, in our case, eating food, a small amount of non-delicious food, reduces the sensation of joy and leads to underproduction of dopamine. Something stagnates in the process of the generation of dopamine in the brain. Genetic damage is called polymorphism. If one of the genes required for the dopamine process is a polymorphed, it will appear in those certain people with prominent symptoms.

Again, dopamine is a neurotransmitter produced by our brain when we enjoy eating. When you enjoy a delicious salad, pot, or slice of pizza, do it because your brain produces a healthy amount of dopamine. So, overeating is forcing us to fix dopamine.

The misconception that fat women have more fun while eating than thin women is flawed. The fMRI again shows that a healthy brain produces much more dopamine than the brain of a food poisoner. Food addiction has the same adverse effects as any other addiction. Addicts developed greater tolerance for the drugs of choice. Low dopamine levels mean less experience with pleasure. Therefore, most addicts consume a significant amount of food when they want to achieve the expected amount of pleasure. This fact is one of the obvious and measurable differences between a naturally lean female brain and an obese female brain.

This phenomenon explains why we act absurdly when we don't reach the food levels that cause the production of dopamine enough to experience pleasure.

Food poisoners suffer overwhelming hunger in the presence of food. Overeating obsessively and compulsively, when not hungry, are more susceptible to smells and a strong desire to eat, even after a full meal. Researchers call this phenomenon "external food hypersensitivity." British Medical Research Centre presents a study in which brain scans have shown how this food susceptibility affects people's diets.

Researchers Andrew Calder, Luca Passamonti, Ph.D., and James Rowe, Ph.D., sought to find out why some people tend to overeat. In the Journal of neuroscience

(January 2011), brain scans of the human were presented to show three sets of images of participants (delicious food, boring food, and irrelevant photos of other subjects). Their response was then recorded.

"People who appear to be more attracted to food have different connections in their brains, '' said obesity expert Marc Andre Cornier, MD, an endocrinologist at the University of Colorado, who has nothing to do with this study.

Dr. Gearhardt von Yale discovered that: "Addictive people respond physiologically, psychologically, and behaviorally to triggers, such as advertising. Very tasty foods are always available and highly marketed today. In the food environment, it is especially important that food-related symptoms can cause pathological reactions." Like drug addicts, food addicts have increased appetite and appetite in response to flood warnings.

You may feel that you are out of control when you eat delicious food, and you lose your strength while eating, and the feeling that you can't help yourself becomes dominant. This is all in stark contrast to naturally lean women who do not even know that this kind of fighting is possible.

Emotional imbalance causes hunger. Take a positive person, whose strongest allergies are everything that influences his optimism, and who eats whenever his energy level is low. The stress is relieved by eating. Also, for uncomfortable feelings, difficult situations, and difficult people, everything out of the sunny comfort zone leads to a trip to the kitchen.

When we are addicted to overeating, our brains are programmed to use food to temporarily relieve anxiety, frustration, stress, depression, agitation, and discomfort with dopamine modification. The longer you use food to improve your mood, the more likely it is that you will be associated with relief from feeling sick with addictive substances. When we experience life's ups and downs with low tolerance, our main coping mechanism is dopamine modification. Emotional imbalance leads to excessive episodes of eating.

CHAPTER 4: WHY WEIGHT LOSS IS TEMPORARY?

Most people who manage to lose weight, gain weight again within a year. This includes people who have taken part in The Biggest Loser or who have their stomachs fixed. This is the most restrained stat in the diet industry. Only 3 out of 100 people who reach the goal can sustain this weight loss beyond the first year.

There is a lesser-known organization called the National Weight Control Registry. The database records people who have been able to maintain more than 30 pounds of weight loss for over 12 months. The organization's goal is to find out why certain people can maintain weight loss while others cannot. In December 2011, in an article published by the New York Times in which all these people were interviewed. Successful dieters shared ways to stay super alert to maintain weight loss. Many of them still need to count calories every day. Some people call the restaurant before eating. The Times reports that weight-keeping efforts for these people are as much effort as losing weight. Even spokespersons of weight loss companies across the have noted that the effort needed to lose weight is as important as the effort taken to lose extra weight.

But let's look at a few facts. There were times in our lives where we didn't have a hard time maintaining a healthy weight. There was a time when we were slim without counting anything. There was a time when you weren't absorbed in food, and there was a time when we weren't forcedly eating. Then I have another question. Why are we different from lean women who do not have this type of dietary habits? What has changed?

Science has made significant progress in figuring out how to achieve long-term weight loss. Flavor-enhanced foods, unreal body images, hectic lifestyles, and chronic diets have changed our brains. We are crazy about food. We use our limited willpower to resist the abundance of attractive foods around us and use our food to calm us as part of our hectic lifestyle. These brain-level changes are documented using brain imaging techniques. Scientists can measure statistically significant differences between obese populations as compared to naturally thin populations. In particular, the study shows that there is a measurable difference between the obese population in the level of activity in the brain area that responds to alterations in thinking and the area responsible for the weighting of the pros and cons of our decision.

The amount of dopamine produced by the brain of obese people is low. Contrary to popular belief, obese people have less pleasure than thin people. Obese people must eat more to experience the same amount of joy. Now that we understand why we need to eat more to get the same amount of dopamine as naturally thin woman's dopamine, let's first talk a little about dopamine. Dopamine is a delightful neurotransmitter, a key chemical that transmits the signals we experience as delight. Dopamine levels are reduced in the brain of overweight people. The amount of joy is much less. These scans show that naturally lean people can experience a higher level of joy when eating the same food than obese people. Despite the widespread misconception that overweight people love food and enjoy it more, the truth is that the more severe the habit of eating is, the fewer food addicts enjoy.

CHAPTER 6: WOMEN ARE DIFFERENT FROM MEN

The basic principles of weight loss are the same for both genders-you burn more calories than you consume- but the factors that lead to a caloric deficit that causes weight loss are not the same. Men and women are different. They are biologically different and emotionally different. These differences are very important because both biology and psychology are important for successful weight loss.

DIFFERENT BODIES

There is no need to explain the physical differences between men and women. The body composition of men and women, that is, the proportions of muscle, bone, and fat that make up the body of men and women are very different. A typical 154-pound man has 69 pounds of muscle, 23 pounds of bone, and 23 pounds of fat (the rest is organs, fluids, etc.). A typical woman weighing 125 pounds weighs 45 pounds of muscle, 15 pounds of bone, and 34 pounds of fat. In summary, men are genetically programmed to have muscular build up with heavier bones than women. Conversely, the female body is designed for higher fat content.

Technically, the definitions of overweight and obesity are based upon the excess body fat (Body Mass Index or BMI is used to categorize the person's weight). Again, the gender is different. Obesity in men is defined as 21-25% body fat and obesity as 25% or more. Obesity in women is defined as 31-33% body fat and obesity as 33% or more. From a biological point of view, men should be lean in appearance, and women should be fat, so men and women of the same size and weight should have very different body compositions. Given the physical differences between sexes in terms of body composition, it is not surprising that body fat recommendations differ between men and women. Men are recommended a range of 12-20% fats, and women are recommended a range of 20-30%. Because of their different body composition, losing weight gives men a biological advantage over women.

DIFFERENT MINDS

Men and women do not share the same physical and psychological build-up. Differences based on emotions between men and women are a very interesting area. John Gray's 1992 book "Men are from Mars, Women are from Venus" attracted people's attention and sparked a debate on the inherent differences between men and women in communication, addressing problems, and causing conflict. Psychologists are not the only ones interested in how mental processes differ between women and men. Much work is also done in the world of basic research. Every year, more and more are learned about the relationship between mental processes and physical functioning, especially concerning neurotransmitters. A 2006 article even states that men smile less than women, were due to how their brains were programmed.

It is well known that chemical behaviors in the brain influence our behaviors in the areas of food and physical activity. Also, although little is known about these signals at this time, there may be differences due to gender. The brain is associated with the potential effects of obesity and gender, so the more we learn about how the brain affects mental health, the more relevant treatment options will be developed. The mental aspect of weight and weight loss cannot be overemphasized. The basic physiology of weight loss is relatively simple. To lose weight, you need to lose more and ingest fewer calories. One needs to know that at the heart of permanent weight loss is the behavior of eating, exercising, and thinking. There is a clear difference between men and women when it comes to weight loss.

HEALTH RISKS FOR OBESE WOMEN

Women and men share the health risks of certain diseases, but some weight-related health problems are found only in women. Weight loss seems to be one of the most important ways for women to overcome these problems beyond the potential health risks. Example:

Polycystic Ovary Syndrome (PCOS) is a condition that can affect a woman's fertility and is associated with obesity. Health professionals recommend weight loss as the first treatment for PCOS because studies have shown that losing weight improves fertility.

Besides, obesity is a risk factor for **Gestational Diabetes**. Studies show that a weight loss of just 10 pounds can significantly reduce a woman's risk of developing gestational diabetes.

Adult obesity and weight gain are also known risk factors for **Postmenopausal Breast Cancer**. In an analysis of a large group of women in Iowa, researchers found that preventing weight gain at childbearing age, or preventing weight gain in overweight women combined with weight loss, was healthy during those years. It was concluded that maintaining a healthy weight reduced the risk of being diagnosed with breast cancer in later years.

Overweight negatively affect the psychological health of both genders but appears to be more emotionally stressful for women (**Emotional Stress**). Studies show that women are less satisfied with weight and overall body shape than men. And most women's dissatisfaction with weight begins early in life and continues into adulthood.

Why? The answer lies, at least partially, in an attachment to the lean body for women in almost all societies.

Weight watcher researchers often hear women say they feel that others are judging them by their appearance (thin and attractive), not by what they are capable of and what they can do. Where do women get this belief? The media is an important source of information. Most of the beautiful women in magazines and big screens are extraordinarily thin people, and for many women, extraordinary thinness is a measure of beauty. This seems to be primarily a woman's problem.

A study that asked men and women for their ideal body shape and asked how they thought of their body in comparison with their ideals was generally satisfied. In contrast, women consistently viewed themselves as heavier than their ideals and expressed a desire to lose weight. Unfortunately, this very thin waif figure is unrealistic (and unhealthy!) And can't be achieved by most women. As a result, many women lose self-esteem and develop a negative body image associated with depression.

So, instead of focusing on being extremely thin, one should focus on maintaining a healthy weight. Now, we will finally move to actual weight loss techniques for losing extra fats. We will be focusing on the root of the problem, the brain.

CHAPTER 7: SELF-HYPNOSIS

At the beginning of this amazing strategy, one can question the individual's ability to be hypnotized. Experts in this field, Ph.D. students, and PhDs who devote their professional lives to hypnosis practice and researchers estimate that 80-90% of the population can be hypnotic.

If you have ever read a book, listened to music, watched plays or movies- you are hypnotized. If your thoughts ever wandered, you forget for a moment if you have heard someone speak your name-you were hypnotized. If you're so engrossed in work that you couldn't think of passing the time, you can get hypnotized. If you fell in love and blinded by the charm of others, you were hypnotized. If you feel "carried" in prayer, you have been hypnotized. As you can see, virtually everyone was hypnotized. All hypnosis is self-hypnosis, with or without the help of a hypnotist.

It is possible that the experience was too spontaneous to even know that it was happening, as in the situation above.

Thus, self-hypnosis is a form, process, or result of self-induced hypnosis. Self-hypnosis is often used as a means of improving the effectiveness of self-indication. In such cases, the subject will play the "double role of the proposer and the proposed to."

There are two important prerequisites before hypnosis:

(1) Sincere wishes: Whenever we are hypnotized, we pass through hidden desires. If you desire to hypnotize yourself, you can easily do it.

(2) Open mind. An open mind does not deny healthy skepticism.

Conservatively assessing the benefits of hypnosis can be difficult. Others in the field are equally enthusiastic. British scientist JBS Haldane writes: "Everyone who even saw a single example of the power of hypnosis and suggestion will comply with how we control its effects and how it could be the face and existence of the world. All we need to do is to understand what can be changed and can be standardized. "For example, use as much as possible in drugs that were once considered magical. "It's a pretty strong statement, but it shows the respect that many knowledgeable scientists have for possible uses of hypnosis. What hypnosis can do for you is depends a lot on what you expect it to be. It's fun rather than ending the hypnosis movement itself, but you practice it as a way to make a difference in yourself. May include the habit of wanting to quit overeating.

You can hope to overcome fear, like the fear of flying. You aspire to relieve headaches, arthritis, dentistry, and birth pains. You may want to overcome insomnia, chronic fatigue, tension, and depression. You may want to become confident in your abilities and become more confident. Much more can be achieved by self-hypnosis. Even those who claim that they don't have the habit of breaking themselves, the anxiety or phobia they want to lose, or the attitude that they have to change, self-hypnosis can benefit them.

Just as the results of hypnotherapies are impressive, the word of warning should be spoken; it's not a great panacea. Hypnosis does nothing that no other cure can achieve. That alone will be faster. But if hypnosis is faster than other forms of treatment, it's not just a self-help program.

Self-help plans are based on best intentions but are not sufficient for many. Well-paved roads are not yellow bricks. Most of us need a boost, a shot of mental adrenaline to get rid of fatigue. We can read a myriad of self-help books and encourage us to think of radiant thoughts, like us, calm down, cheer us up, or relax in any way to improve ourselves. But that doesn't seem to be enough.

Hypnosis offers something more. It does not only create a climate of relaxation. This allows you to think in a focused manner. Most importantly, it enhances the state of our consciousness and shifts a kind of mental channel to a higher level. This increased state of consciousness allows a connection to the unconscious rather than the unconscious sleepless state itself. When you practice hypnosis, you are not overlooked, but you are in contact with the subconscious. And it makes the difference between hypnosis and other approaches to self-improvement.

CHAPTER 8: CONDITIONS FOR HYPNOSIS TO WORK OUT

Although hypnosis itself cannot be accurately predicted, clinical experience and laboratory experiments at institutions such as Harvard and Stanford suggest that those who are most susceptible to hypnosis tend to share certain characteristics. As already mentioned, virtually everyone can benefit from hypnosis. However, if you have most of these characteristics, studies have shown that you may be easier to hypnotize than others. Here are some of the criteria for hypnosis:

1. Motivation

The motivation is at the top of the list. If you don't want to be hypnotized, you won't. If you are strong enough to change something, the chance is to be able to hypnotize yourself. But such motives must come from within. You need to want to change yourself, not because other people think you should, but because it's what you need at the moment.

2. Optimism

Top people tend not to be skeptics if you take a continuum of hypnosis from low to high. This doesn't mean you can't hypnotize yourself if you're skeptical now. However, we hope that by the end of this topic, your skepticism will be alleviated somewhat so that you can experience hypnosis more easily. It turns out that most hypnotic people are likely to have a hopeful and optimistic view of life. To them, the bottle is not half empty but half full.

3. Defending

The people most susceptible to hypnosis are usually lawyers. This is an extension of buoyancy, trust, and hope reflected in their optimism. Whether it's something new in medicine, politics, art, or something that interests them, they are keen to spread the word. Opposite is a person who is very cognitive and very scientific in her evaluation. This individual demand evidence wants to read half a dozen books and scrutinizes the subject before committing himself. This attitude of the brain is not wrong. It simply means that such reality-oriented individuals must stay longer in hypnosis to get results.

4. Concentration

An important feature of hypnosis is increased concentration. Hypnosis deepens your concentration, but you need it to achieve this condition. The more distracting a person is, the more he responds if he tries to hypnotize himself or is hypnotized by others. He also has to use this method more often to make a profit. Meanwhile, most people at least sometimes have a deep focus. Go to the room when they are reading and call their name. You can't get the answer. Those people can't hear your voice because they are too concentrated. We find no significant evidence difference between vigorous situation and self-hypnosis itself.

5. Acceptability

Many people are afraid to be hypnotized so as not to be absorbed in the will of others. This may be called Svengali syndrome. A mysterious stranger with a black cloak and flint's eyes seizes the soul of a naked girl while bending her will to adapt to an embarrassing wish. People who are prone to hypnosis have normal or good intelligence and a core of beliefs and firm attitudes that are fundamental to life. An example of such a person is someone with a well-trained religious education that embraces new ideas. He is hard to be fooled. He is sensitive to wise suggestions. Of course, the receptivity level differs from person to person. The receptivity for new ideas is one of the determinants of how easily you can get hypnosis. On a scale of 0-5 (0 is a person impervious to hypnosis), the majority of the population falls in the middle, for example, in the range 2 to 3. However, rest assured that your level of susceptibility to hypnosis is not included in the five-point scale. At the age of two or three, hypnosis should be repeated more often. However, being at the top of the scale has both disadvantages and benefits.

6. Imagination

Scientists at the Hypnosis Institute at Stanford University School of Psychology have been studying the hypnotic differences between individuals for nearly two decades. This is a project supported by the National Mental Health Institute and the Air Force Office of Scientific Laboratory. An organization that does not tend to fund trivial efforts. Dr. Josephine R. Hilgard, a clinical professor of psychiatry at Stanford University, reported on the study: For some reason, people who have been imaginatively active as a child can have hypnosis. The theory states that the imagination and ability to participate in adventures that emerged early in life remained alive and functional through continued use. Among university students, reading, drama, creativity, childhood imagination, religion, sensory, and thirst for adventure were activities identified as hypnosis. Hypnosis is deeply involved in one or more imaginary areas (reading novels, listening to music, experiencing the aesthetic of nature, adventuring the body and mind) can do. "

Dr. Hilgard found that the student in major of humanities is most susceptible to hypnosis, the majors of social sciences are comparatively less, and students of natural sciences and engineering are not much hypnotized. The experience and research of other employees in this area tend to corroborate Stanford University results. According to Dr. Lewis R. Wolberg, a 40-year authority in the field: people with the ability to enjoy sensory stimulations and can adapt themselves to different roles have more tendency to be hypnotic than others.

Dr. Hilgard's lab was the most vulnerable to those who had fictitious friends in childhood and could read, adventure, and be immersed in nature. Suspicious, withdrawn, and hostile people have discovered that they tend to resist hypnosis. "Few people appreciate all of the above criteria. You don't even have to show improvement in all areas. You can make up for what's missing in another category. Defined these criteria, Hypnosis still needs a great deal of research, and it has been accepted by the academic and medical community as a subject worthy of serious investigation. A lot of eye-widening results are drawn from the research.

CHAPTER 9: CAN YOU BE HYPNOTIZED OR NOT?

Earlier evidence suggests that the presence of these criteria contributes to hypnosis, but there is no specific way to predict who can or cannot do hypnosis. Ernest R. Hilgard, husband of Dr. Josephine R. Hilgard, mentioned above, is a professor of psychology and director of the Stanford Research Institute for Hypnosis Research, say that hypnotic vulnerability, there is no guarantee of this. At least two studies (including our own) agree that normal subjects are more hypnotized than subjects exposed to neurosis or overt neurosis.

This helps fix the common image that hypnosis is a sign of weakness and instability. Dr. Roger Bernhardt talked about his patient in his book 'Self-mastery through Self-hypnosis' that "He was a patient and head of his department, a professor at Boston. He made quick and effective progress on his analysis, and then on some small work issues, he thought hypnosis would help. This man had the standards of high sensitivity: he tends to trust, pause judgment, confront perspective or cause, tend to live in the present. He was good. He had a sharp memory, with the ability to concentrate well, he was receptive to new ideas, but he has a hardcore of his own beliefs. Yet, he was not hypnotizable at every point of the test I gave him. It was difficult. Ultimately, I believe that one knows that someone can be hypnotized after he is hypnotized. The Boston professor was a member of a small population who was less likely to experience hypnosis (such helplessness can be temporary)."

But as a reader, you are likely to be among the majority of people who can hypnotize themselves. Let's say you are innocent in what you otherwise cannot prove. Just once try acting upon these points:

1. Follow the hypnosis steps (will be explained later) and believe that you are hypnotizing your abilities at this point.

2. Give yourself the implant you want to change or improve.

3. Repeat the process religiously, knowing that each experience adds to the cumulative benefit.

Many practitioners, including myself, see self-hypnosis as a cognitive skill that allows both learning and sharpening. If you don't hypnotize at first, try tomorrow, tomorrow, and tomorrow. I'm convinced that nine out of ten readers of this book can learn with the determination and patience to hypnotize the fastest and easiest methods I know. However, there are simple experiments that can determine if you are likely to be hypnotized, which can also be a rough indication of your sensitivity to hypnosis. This is called the eye roll test, and it only takes a few seconds.

Herbert Spiegel, a clinical professor of psychiatry for physicians and surgeons at Columbia University, examined 2,000 subjects to test a paper that most hypnotics can curl their eyes to the heads. Conversely, anyone who cannot apply hypnosis cannot lookup. "Commonly seen."

Dr. Spiegel writes: "When a person wants to concentrate and stay undisturbed, one attitude is to look up. Sometimes they close their eyes. This trick is a consciousness of the surroundings to call attention. The role test is an extension of that. In about 75% of the 2,000 consecutive cases, a 5-second test predicted hypnotic transformation capacity.

The percentage of hypnotized subjects tested positive for the eye-roll test. This ability to look at your eyes to head is considered by some researchers to be a neurological phenomenon. It occurs in some people but not in others. It is virtually certain that this person is not hypnotized if he is looking straight after eye roll test. To run the test yourself:

1. Keep your head still while looking straight.

2. Don't move your head look up at your eyebrows, and then look up at the top of your head.

3. With your eyes raised, slowly close the eyelids.

4. Open the eyelids and normally focus again.

You can decide for yourself whether your eyes will look up during the test. If you are looking at the ceiling, the eye roller worked, and you can hypnotize. Despite your efforts, it doesn't work if you're still looking at the wall in front of you or something at eye level. You can still benefit from exercise, but the possibility is that you do not experience the increased state of self-hypnosis.

CHAPTER 10: HOW TO PERFORM SELF-HYPNOSIS?

There is nothing sacred about how to cause hypnosis-achieving your goal is the most important thing, not the way you take it. Guidance technology does not guarantee greater success than any others. However, some methods work faster and are easier to execute than others, which makes them more practical. The technique I like to teach in this book is quick and easy.

The first thing you should do to prepare for practicing self-hypnosis is to know whether it is a habit you want to break or the goal you want to achieve, or another aspect of your existence, physical or internal. The setting to change is decided. You can still benefit from exercise without a specific purpose, but the way you learn here is tailored to meet your goals, and perhaps more people will dig into something and find something else. Because they can, they are not completely satisfied. I want to use self-hypnosis to make a certain change in myself.

Just as you learn new skills and games, you must first thoroughly learn the basics of self-hypnosis. You can also use abbreviations if you are familiar with the technique and can practice it well. Once you have learned the rules first, you can design the exercises to suit your needs and personality. But before writing a book, why not let's learn the alphabet first.

Over time, you'll be able to work out almost anywhere, including offices, restaurants, trains, and planes. However, for the easiest learning and confidence in its use, you must first practice in a relatively quiet and secluded location. Ideally, armchairs, especially those with footrests and those that can recline partially. your chosen site must be a place where you feel comfortable and uninterrupted by yourself. Initially, each session should take a few minutes before getting used to the technique. After several learning sessions, each experience should not exceed 1 minute. Even in this short time, it will quickly be reduced to 30 seconds.

The main reason for the lengthy initial sessions is that relaxation is an important prelude to hypnosis, and you need to learn to relax. You might think you already know how to relax, but if you're not a very slim minority, you aren't. Some people are "relaxing" and watching movies on the golf course or the Game Bridge. Such pursuits are challenging and even pressure of our stressful work life and even the necessary distractions from everyday life. But this is not relaxing as we mean by hypnosis. As used herein, "relaxed" means free from any kind of mental and physical pressure. Such a situation is easier to clarify than to achieve.

You need to relax for two reasons. The ultimate relaxation is when you are in a deep sleep. It is an end in itself, a relaxing balm for the body and mind. Moreover, the relaxation used in hypnosis paves the way for unconsciousness, making it easier to accept and implement suggestions.

Described in a useful guide by Hermann S. Schwartz. Art of Relaxation: the best result of continuous auto-suggestion is achieved when mental censorship is unprepared and in full relaxation. Then our thoughts are free to get into the subconscious."

First, make yourself as comfortable as possible. We assume there is a footrest on which you can rest your feet. They should rest side by side and not intersect a few centimeters apart. Keep your arms still, with your left arm on your chair's left arm and your right arm on the right arm of the chair. Then tilt your head back and lean against the headrest or back of your chair.

You are not yet relaxed. Relaxing your entire body is harder than you think unless you're careful. We avoid syncope and focus on relaxing parts of the body at once. Start with your left foot placed on the footrest. Lift your foot a few inches from the footrest, hold it in the air for a few seconds, and pull your foot back up from its weight to the footrest. Right foot after a break. Raise your right foot three to four inches and let it stay there for a few seconds and put it back in the chair. Now imagine that you are lifting your left foot into the air without removing it from the footrest. There is a slight tension in the legs, slight tension in the legs. you must feel relaxed. Imagine lifting your right foot in the air with your right foot on the footrest. It is another slight tension, be relaxed.

Then go to your left arm. Lift your arm a few inches in the air, hold it for a few seconds, and then let it die back to your armrest. Do the same for the right arm. Move it a few inches away from the armrest and take it back into the armrest. Leave your left arm on the armrest, but imagine raising your arm. You will have a little tension in your arm. Be relaxed. Repeat the mental image of lifting your right arm a few inches in the air, keeping your right arm on the chair arm. Release this tension and relax.

Now turn to your waist. Pull your belly down, take the back off your chair, grab it, and let it fall. Staying there, you'll feel a slight tension in the middle section, just as if you were just getting up. Then, move your shoulders and chest away from your chair, and then let them sit down for a while. Imagine you're a little tensed up as you are pulling back from your chair, leaving your shoulders and chest unmoved. Stop and relax.

Finally, the head. Remove it from the headrest or back of the chair and move it forward a few inches to flush it back. Imagine that. Feel that there is a slight tension in your neck. be relaxed. Tense all facial muscles without moving your head. Tighten and pull facial features to relax. A slight tension in your face moving to your eyes through nose and mouth and then released all the tension.

Your whole body is now relaxed and heavier. From head, face, and neck to shoulders and chest and arms, and from the center to legs and feet, the whole body is heavy and warm and sinks directly into the chair. Enjoy this heavy, warm, and relaxing atmosphere. Your body seems to be sinking down and down the chair. Now let's look at the deployment process. There are three stages to this, and counting up to three must be done.

ONE: Your eyes are on your eyebrows as high as you can get them. Take a look at the top of your head.

TWO: While your eyes are still looking up, take a deep breath, and slowly close your eyelids.

THREE: Exhale. Relax your eyes. Let your body relax as if it is floating.

As you can see, when you count, do one thing. With two, you do two things, close your eyes and take a deep breath. Then count three things in three: exhale, relax your eyes, and lift your body.

It's very relaxing, and it's a lot of fun to feel like you're floating directly on this armchair. Treat yourself now in this comfort and go on a short imaginary vacation. Imagine where you have been, where you want to go, where you can feel total peace and peace with yourself and the world.

Many people lie on a quiet beach, seeing the sun warm, the cool breeze blowing, and the waves gently rolling up. Others imagine a remote hideaway in the woods. Imagine you are enjoying a large warm pool. Pick your vacation location and see yourself there. Fantasize whatever is soothing and pleasure-giving to you. Imagine yourself in a comfortable place of your choice, and your body will float further down the chair. Your body is now a little detached from you. Now you can give the body instructions on how to live. It is advisable to provide him with 3 step instructions in the form of a triplet.

The first step. "overeating is poison to my body, not to me."

Second step. "I need my body to live well."

Third step. "As long as I want to live, I protect my body just as I need protect -------," and here you say the name of the person you love. It can be a child, a parent, a loved one, or a pet. To have the highest emotional power, it must be someone near you who's happiness affects you deeply.

However, some readers may not feel strong about everyone or may have vague feelings about the closest person. If you have such a question, it's best to omit "... how I protect" and end the three-fold reasoning with "... protect my body".

After the three-step rationale, I recommend improving the experience of self-hypnosis while at the same time strengthening the verbal implants suggested during exercise. When I say numerous involvements every day, it's a work adaptation of what I say, but usually not for fantasy purposes. I recommend you use your fantasies and make them work for you. To explain: When our unconstrained thoughts are allowed to wander, they remind us of the scene, not the words. When thinking about your schedule for this weekend, don't say, "I'm going to a good dinner and then to the movie I wanted to see."

You should introduce your favorite restaurant instead. You should picture the scene as there is a pleasant and relaxed atmosphere. The waiter will bring your favorite food and present it to you. There is a faint scent, and you can enjoy the taste. Then watch yourself in a darkened theater. The seats are gorgeous and comfortable, and it would be great fun to be in the movie. Such thoughts, such short and fun flights from reality, more accurately reflect our original selves than words. After all, people thought clearly in the photos before creating words to explain their thoughts. Images, therefore, go deeper into us and are more emotionally involved because they are more lively and powerful than words.

As used in self-hypnosis, the image embodies a syllogism skeleton. Operandi mode is simple. The syllogism forms the framework. Then dress it with a picture. Imagine yourself who is strong, confident, and satisfied with yourself and the world around you. If you want to be a controlled eater, imagine a situation where you had food in your mouth or plate and are now completely satisfied. If overeating is a problem, look slim and attractive and enjoy reaching for a glass of water instead of a slice of chocolate cake. And so on. The purpose of applying self-hypnosis naturally determines which image to use.

In explaining some of these specific goals, I suggest a suitable type of image for everyone. We recommend that you consider your situation based on your personality, experience, and lifestyle. I offer a paradigm. Change the shape to suit your needs. I think it's very important to use this image as a complement to the syllogism. Not only does it give an emotional wallop to the logic of the triad, but it also provides an alternative to the triad. If time allows, the two are first used sequentially in a two-stage implant. The image fills the triple logic. Later, you may want to switch back and forth for brevity and versatility. During the 30 second exercise, you should only include the unconscious verbally and after a few hours only visually. This serves as an excuse to avoid monotony. You can give up on self-hypnosis before a positive result is felt. Besides, focusing on the image answers the complaints of some people who may be protesting the intellectual nature of the syllogism. Some of the patients said that they were too intelligent to give us something we could only feel. Such people can enjoy greater reward through images than the more cerebral approach of three-stage reasoning.

In summary, the following is recommended: you will start by including both syllogism and image in the self-hypnosis exercise. Let's make one to the other. Try a fair process and find what you feel is right for you. Stick to both, get involved either orally or visually, or switch between the two. After becoming a seasoned hypnotist, it's easy to decide what is best for you.

After self-image, you can make post-hypnotic suggestions: attitudes or behaviors that you want to move into daily life after you escape self-hypnosis. If you want to be a thin person, then think about the feeling you will have with the thin body whenever you feel like eating more than it is needed. You also tell yourself that if you become a master of your body and not vice versa, you will feel calm and comfortable and have a feeling of self-satisfaction.

After focusing on the three elements of the three-stage logic, dealing with mental images, and making post-hypnotic suggestions, you are ready to escape self-hypnosis. To do this, count from 3 to 1 in silent mode.

THREE. Be prepared.

TWO. Round your eyes up with the eyelids closed.

ONE. Open the eyelids slowly. Then fasten your fists by hand, spread your fingers widely, and yawn at the same time. And it's real self-hypnosis, without hobgoblins and Svengali trap.

I will warn you again. Don't be surprised if the earth doesn't move in this experience. Individual answers are different. You may feel a strong and distinct functional feeling at a level that is completely different from your normal state of consciousness. At the other extreme, you can feel a little relaxed, such as a relaxing break. If so, don't be discouraged.

Repeat the exercises as often as possible (ideally every few hours) using the procedure described here. Expect results to be achieved and believe that something in your subconscious mind is going to make the changes you want. After all, you have a lot to do. The suggestions you make take the form of three-stage reasoning. The syllogism is the foundation of logic that has contributed well to humans for over 2000 years. As Aristotle said, "Syllogism is a discourse when something is inevitably followed by something else.

Consider the logic of the three elements of the triple logic used during self-hypnosis.

1. "To my body ... overeating is poisonous." That's a fact. An American general surgeon, your own doctor, will tell you.

2. "You need your body to live." Is there any discussion?

3. * Protect your body to the extent you want to live, just like a person you love. "

Your body needs the care to live. Overeating puts your body into danger. The choice is yours: you have a protected body or a lot of food (and not). It's logical, simple, and impregnable.

Moreover, this method of self-hypnosis for self-help takes the positive attitude of "doing" rather than "not." For example, if you break your overeating habits, you will focus on the positive effect of respecting your body and protecting it from harm. Since childhood, we have been conditioned to respond favorably to "do" rather than "do not."

A pioneer and teacher of this method. Herbert Spiegel wrote in the International Journal of Clinical and Experimental Hypnosis: If a patient accepts the obligation to respect his body, he will be distracted from the urge to eat. He is currently experiencing two impulses at the same time. It is the urge to eat or the urge to protect the body. By holding them together and emphasizing respect for his body, he ignores the urge to eat. The urge to be repeatedly unsatisfied and neglected eventually disappears. "

In addition to emphasizing affirmation, another major advantage of this method is its simplicity. People don't have long sessions to prepare and fear: "I have to experience this long again." It only takes a few seconds, so there is no excuse for its length or energy expenditure to avoid exercise. It's human nature to find an easy way, so keep it short and concise. This is also compatible with our unconscious understanding, as it does not know the time. Quickly and easily give unknowingly acceptable ideas.

I was talking about adjusting exercises to suit my personality. Remember that you are hypnotized. This book provides you with tools and shows you how to use them. Once you learn how to use them, it's up to you what you do with them.

As an example, let's take a look at the first line of the reasoning. "overeating is poison to my body, not to me." The word "poison" is very relevant, especially when it is related to eating uncontrollably. But after a while, you may find that other words of your development affect you more. The word "cancer" has a particular meaning for healthcare professionals. The word "cancer" is also very effective for people who have had this disease with their friends and family because it can cause a sort of shock. (I assume that if the subject turns his thoughts to his relatives or friends out of the question, it does not adversely affect how that happens).

Another word that often appears instead of "poison" is "catastrophic." This is a word that can cover a wide range of complaints. Excessive drinking is catastrophic. Insomnia is devastating. Erectile dysfunction is devastating.

It is neither necessary nor recommendable to choose a phrase and stick to it permanently. I change myself. I use the word "cancer," the word "poison," and the word "catastrophic." By switching between the three, you can see that your thoughts are fresh and vibrant. Choose the metaphor that you feel most comfortable with and seems most important to you.

The problem of omission of interpretation or condensation in the case of syllogism in analysis and self-hypnosis is very different from the frequency of practice. The use of abbreviations is useful when it is convenient for you. However, if hypnosis is applied infrequently, it works in reverse and results slower.

Dr. Roger Bernhard wrote that he once visited his mom at the hospital who had a broken hip and had several surgeries. She endured some pain as expected from such surgery, and he tried hypnosis with her for a few months. When he visited her again, she said, "I exercise every two hours!" And it's in the 80s.

So, it can be maintained that age is not a retarding factor if you want to practice hypnosis. You can do it whenever you want. All you have to do is to stay persistent and be optimistic.

If the problem of being attacked is sufficiently threatened, one does not have to hesitate to practice every 2-3 hours. You can always do it before bedtime, enough to prepare for healthy sleep as part of the ritual. You have strong technology and want to be as successful as possible. Take maximum challenges to ensure this success.

You might wonder why there is a difference between "me" and "my body" in the first expression of the practicing self-hypnosis. "For my body. Not for me, but my body. "The reason behind using these words is that your body is not you. These words are not synonymous with each other. You consist of several parts, one of which is your body. By distinguishing between the two, your body must adapt to everything you give. Objectivity is explained while differentiating between these two, and if you choose to be a keeper and protector, you will step back and look passionately at your body. It gives you the opportunity and provides the same warmth and care you give to your child or someone. Near you, this setting is very beneficial to you.

Now, let's say you have carefully followed all the instructions. Relaxed They maximized the state of self-hypnosis. Presented a specific goal to the syllogistic reasoning, you did all these 7 to 8 times a day. But nothing seems to happen. You still have the nasty symptoms you want to lose. In this case, three suggestions might help.

(1) It seems to have no consequences, but I believe something is happening behind the scene. I Insist to continue it.

(2) Check your motives and, if justified, check once again.

(3) Memorize Not only the three-stage logic and repeat the words like a parrot without thinking or feeling. You must be mindful of what are you saying?

Let's deal with these points in order:

(1) Endurance

If you do this exercise regularly, the results may not appear for a while, but there will always be progress. The plane will move forward even if it is covered with clouds. If you're not stationary in this cloud bank, you can't see it, but the plane is moving forward. After all, it bursts from the clouds into the sunshine. Still, that direction is not always exactly north. A deep understanding of the human mind reveals ups and downs. Progress tends to move forward but not continuously: Two in the front and one in the back.

(2) Motivation

If you don't get a positive result, test your motivation, and look at it from two perspectives. How motivated is your self-hypnosis experience, and how much you want to achieve your goals?

Regarding the first question, when you join an exercise, do you want to quickly get over it and continue your life, or do you want to pay attention to everything for 30 seconds? There is a world of difference between the two situations. You may, like a robot, perform abdominal exercises, much like moving the forefinger up and down in the morning with no consequences. However, doing exercises simultaneously with full focus and participation can make a big difference.

So, it's hypnosis. Paradoxically, concentration is a goal, and a means to achieve that goal. We use hypnosis to achieve higher concentrations, but we need to focus our attention to succeed. Paradoxically, that's how it works.

The other aspect of motivation, the deepness you want to change, spans the range of intensities. For example, a drunken man may feel stumbled at home and see a discouraged look on his son's face, causing him to lose respect. This can help his self-proposal to get rid of his alcohol problems. There is a 180-degree difference between such a person and those who say, "I am trying because my rich uncle wants it." Such a motive does not reach his stomach, unlike someone who says: "I lose my son's respect, so I have to overcome it. It makes more sense to me than life itself." He is trying to give up his life but gives up the idea when he witnesses the disrespect in his son's eye. Motivation Your motive does not have to lead to a life or death decision, but it should still be strong if you want to achieve positive results.

(3) Feeling

Try to change the expressions sometimes to protect yourself from the hollow three-word logic. The opening part has already proposed switching words such as "poison," "cancer," and "ruinous." Next, in the third part of the three-stage logic, the subject says, "Protect your body (or mental health or whatever it works for) as long as you want to live." To give the term a boost, we need to add the names of people who are very close.

For example, there was a man who severely injured his face in his daughter's car accident. He had to keep dabbing his blood while he waited for the surgeon to come to her. Recalling this experience increases his respect for his daughter and has a great influence on his three-stage logic.

Another example is Helen's example, which has been witnessed only once. She showed weight problems. She weighed 200 pounds, given or taken some. She was taught hypnosis, and since then, she had been in regular contact with the hypnotist. She and her husband traveled a lot. she used to call the doctor to let him know what she was doing. It was helpful for the patient to see a physician who recommends a diet for weight loss. Helen did it. A diet was developed that recommended the consumption of 500 calories a day less than she was used to and losing one pound a week.

She called the doctor every month. Yes, she lost a pound a week, which was slow and painful. She wondered how she could cope with the suffering she endured when she was "hungry." If hypnosis was successful, she wasn't supposed to be so hungry and lacking something. One day she called the doctor that she has an adult son who was traveling to India. It showed she was worried about her son, who was doing a pretty dangerous job. The doctor was quite impressed that there was a way there that could immediately (a) induce motivation and (b) reduce pain. Since then, she had included the idea of her son in a three-stage logic.

So, the third step is to protect your body to the extent I want to live. Rather than just telling how she was, "She added, how I protect my son." she said over the phone that her recent reduced food intake was not accompanied by a feeling of distress?"

I would like to point out that such a coder should have been included in the practice from the beginning, but it was not. Importantly, this addition to this motivation had an emotional impact on her self-implications for weight management. As suggested, she kept meditating on the matter, recalling the feelings she had about her son and his safety and wondering why she should not give her body the same respect and protection. In the last report, she was within £ 20 of her goal.

Therefore, it should be emphasized that it is desirable to say only words and omit thoughts and feelings. Our self-hypnosis exercise deals with two concepts. It is a mixture of cold three-stage logic and warm subjective emotions. When distillate is finally filtered, it is certainly intoxicating.

While learning self-hypnosis, perform muscle relaxation exercises before the introduction. Once you have mastered self-hypnosis, you can remove temporary muscle relaxation and complete your session in 30 seconds. It's a good idea to reread the instructions earlier in this chapter to create both relaxation and hypnosis and practice until you get used to it. You can also record and play the instructions until you understand the technique.

CHAPTER 11: OVERCOMING NEGATIVE HABITS

Fortunately, most of our days have a sort of "groove." Actions in a plan that you perform with little thought are performed almost automatically. Otherwise, our lives become tediously complicated, and we spend a lot of time figuring out how to tie our shoes, prepare our meals, go to work, and more. In this way, we can carry out our daily routines with almost no thought and focus our attention on more demanding activities. Repetitive work in life becomes a habit.

Habits can also be undesirable, and these grooves are deeply rooted in today's patterns. They are against us because they waste our time. For example, if you know that you have a limited amount of time to get to work after waking up in the morning, you'll notice that in the middle of breakfast you'll find the morning paper at the table, pick it up, and usually spend the next hour studying. Spend In the daily news, you could spend a good deal of the rest of your time explaining delays or looking for new jobs.

By the way, in our discussion of habits, we call them "desired" or "undesired" rather than "good" or "bad." The words "good" and "bad" have moral implications. These mean certain decisions. In the example cited in the paragraph above, reading a newspaper is not morally "bad," but not desirable at this time.

The terms "desired" and "undesirable" are the terms "ego," meaning self-determination, not decisions made externally. As with psychoanalysis, our goal is to push material from the "conscience" camp into the "ego" realm.

In many cases, you may even say that removing unnecessary habits requires more than a simple choice. You may want to consciously discard your habits, but fulfilling a wish is a very different matter. There are several reasons for this. First, habits are inherent in their definition and are deeply rooted in their behavior, so they are reflected without thinking. Just thinking "I don't do" does not necessarily affect us deep enough to stop unwanted behavior.

The longer the habit we have with us, the more often we do it, the more secure it will be, and the harder it will be to wipe it off. Please quit overeating. It is not uncommon to start eating without knowing it when already taken a full meal or when absorbed in conversation or work. Such behaviors are driven into individual behavioral patterns dozens of times a day, daily, and over ten years, actually becoming a second cortex that is as natural as breathing (ironically, overcoming eating habits are becoming increasingly difficult for people).

Such habits have physical-neurologic-foundation. The neural pathways in our body can be compared to unpaved roads. This road is smooth before vehicles drive on dirt roads. When a car first rides on the road, its tires leave marks, but the ruts are flat. Rain and wind can easily pass by and smooth the road again. However, after 100 rides with deeper and deeper tires, rain and wind make little impression on the deep ruts. They stay there.

The same applies to people. To expand the metaphor a little, we were born with a smooth street in our heads. When a young child first buttons a jacket or ties a shoe, the effort is tedious, clumsy, and frustrating. More trials are needed until the child gets the hang of it, and a successful move becomes a behavioral pattern.

From a physiological point of view, these movement instructions travel along nerve paths to the muscles and back again. The message is sent to the central nervous system along an afferent pathway. The "I want to lift my legs" impulse continues in the efferent pathway from the central nervous system to my muscles: "Raise my legs." After a while, such messages are automatically enriched by countless repetitions and automatically sent at electrical speed.

Return to the car and the street. Suppose the car decides to avoid a worn groove and take a new path. What's going on the car will go straight back into the old ditch. Like people trying to get out of old habits, they tend to revert to old habits.

Still, we haven't developed any unwanted habits. We learn them, and we can rewind the learning. It can be unconditional. And here, self-hypnosis takes place, pushing the individual out of the established habit gap in a smooth manner of new behavior.

The advantage it offers compared to simple willpower trial and error results from an increase in the state of consciousness that characterizes the state of self-hypnosis. As a neurological phenomenon in itself, this elevated state of consciousness appears to elevate the individual over previous behavioral patterns. A further extension of the unpaved road analogy is that the hovercraft slides a few centimeters above the road, over a rut or habit. Regardless of the habit of working, the implementation process is the same. Only the verbal implant and the image below are different. To encapsulate the induction process, count one, for one thing, two for two things and count three for three things:

1. Please raise your eyes as high as possible.

2. Still staring, slowly close your eyes and take a deep breath.

3. Exhale, relax your eyes, and float your body. Then, if time permits, spend a little more time and introduce yourself to the most comfortable, calm, and pleasant place in your imagination.

Now, when you float deep inside the resting chair, you will feel a little away from your body. It's another matter, so you can give her instructions on how to behave.

At this point, the specific purpose of self-hypnosis determines the expression and image content of the syllogism. It provides suggestions for discussing different habits that can be followed as shown or modified as needed. This strategy can help overcome the habit of overeating.

Overall, we are a country boasting abundant food. Most of us (with the blatant and lamentable exception) have enough money to make sure we are comfortably overeating. As a result, many of us get obese. So, the weight loss business is a big industry. Tablet makers, diet developers, and exercise studios will not confuse customers who want to lose weight.

It is said that every fat person who has a hard time escaping has lost weight. Unfortunately, too often, the lean man spends his life, nevertheless never succeeding in his escape. Despite the image of a funny fat man, everyone rarely enjoys being overweight- most people become unhappy, rarely so confident, and less than confident and ruining their lives. Obesity seems to creep on only some of us, and by the time we notice it, it is a painful habit to overeat or eat, like the excess weight itself.

Self-hypnosis can help this lean man release his bond of "too hard" and start a new life. An article in the International Journal of Clinical and Experimental Hypnosis (January 1975) reports on such cases. Sidney E. and Mitchell P. Pulver cite family doctors study hypnosis in medical and dental practice.

Dr. Roger Bernhardt, while mentioning one of his overweight patients, said that "I brought the patient to the hospital for about a year and a half ago. She went to many doctors to cut back. She said she was rarely leaving home because she was extremely obese; she was relaxing and avoiding people. She came in for £ 380. I started trans in my first session. She continued on a diet and focused on telling her she would like people when she lost weight. She came for the first three or four sessions each week, after which I started teaching her self-hypnosis. Now, this woman lost a total of £ 150, but beyond that, she became another person. She was virtually introverted and rarely came out of her home. She dared to do a part-time job in cosmetics. She hosts a party to show off her cosmetics and hypnotizes herself before the party. She became the state's second-largest saleswoman and earned tens of thousands of dollars."

Simply put, here are the therapies you should use when using self-hypnosis for weight management. After provoking self-hypnosis, mentally recite the syllogism. "I need my body alive. To the extent I want to live, I protect my body just as I protect it."

In the case of a tie mate picture, one can imagine himself in two situations where he is likely to overeat: between meals and at the dining table. With his eyes closed, he imagines a movie screen on the wall. He is on the screen himself, in every situation he finds when he is reading, chatting with others, watching TV, or having trouble calorie counting.

Instead of reaching for popcorn, potato chips, or peanuts as before, he is now simply focusing on the conversation, the television screen, or the printed page, perhaps except for a glass of water, and I congratulate you on being unfamiliar with anything at the table.

The second scene that catches your eye is the dining table. Do you tend to grab this second loaf? Instead, put your hand on your forehead and remember, "Protect my body." Looking at a cake, a loaf, a potato, or a cake raises the idea, "This is for someone. I'm good enough". With the fork down, take a deep breath and be proud to help one-person flow through the body.

Then, imagine a very simple and effective exercise method that simply puts your hand on the edge of the table and pushes it. Better yet, stand up from the chair and leave the table at this point.

Here's another image I'd recommend to a self-hypnotist. If you introduce yourself to the screen of this fictional movie, you will find yourself slim. Give yourself the ideal line that you want to see to others. Cut the abdomen and waistline to the desired ratio. Take an imaginary black pencil, sketch the entire picture, and make the lines sharp and solid. Hold photo Because you can keep this slender picture, you can lose weight.

Then get out of your hypnosis and repeat it regularly every few hours. Exercise is especially useful during the temptation to be used as a comfortable, calorie-free substitute for fatty snacks or as an additional serving with meals. It would be a good time to practice it just before dinner.

As a complement to this discussion, Dr. Roger Bernhardt, while talking about a patient, wrote:" I would like to touch on one of my patients, Mr. Happiness. (He often said to me, so he has this name in my reasoning: "All I want from life is being happy.")

Happiness and I have had many problems together, including my sister's suicide, a heart attack, the end of his previous business, and the establishment of a new business. But now I'm glad to say; he's a happy retired man. He says he comes every 6 to 8 weeks, "to keep the wheels oiled."

Shortly after becoming familiar with hypnosis, I enthusiastically talked to him about it and invited him to use it to treat current problems. He refused. He was afraid of that. After a while, I wrote a small brochure about hypnosis. One day, I handed a copy to Mr. Happiness. A few weeks later, he said, "Oh, that's funny. It's not psychoanalysis, but he says that all you do is ..." and he repeated the steps of the deployment process. It was

"Yes," I replied, "It's a simple one to two. Do you want to do that?"

Again, he refused: "Oh, not me!"

This issue has not been raised again for several months. It must be mentioned that Mr. Happiness was a fat man and was instructed to lose weight for a heart attack. But what the battle: these potatoes, these rich desserts, and these knives! Then one day, he said to me, "I have done something I recently thought you might be interested in. When I go to bed at night, I count, one, two, three, and I say: I don't eat anything, I just drink grapefruit juice, but I still feel well filled. Patient in the letter: "I only count three.")

He then confessed to me that for the last few months, he had done this. He lost weight and felt comfortable doing it. Still, he didn't want me to hypnotize him.

This is, of course, the beauty of self-hypnosis. He didn't have to be hypnotized: he was able to hypnotize himself to accomplish what he wanted. We can do the same. All we need to do is to believe in what we are suggesting to ourselves and feel the power.

CHAPTER 12: THE CRITICAL COMPONENT OF SELF-HYPNOSIS

You have it-practically everything I know about the practice of self-hypnosis. As you learned in this book, the technique of defining it and using it for self-therapy is very simple, as the condition may define or understand itself.

This triple sided weapon-self-imaging-post-hypnotic suggestion provides the fastest cure that brings me to mind and body changes. There is even clinical evidence that better results can be achieved without the support of others. A few years ago, John Clifford-Luck experimented at Stanford University with both self-hypnosis and hetero hypnosis (Hypnotic state induced by another person).

In summary, he summarized his results: "... self-hypnosis without prior hypnosis is as effective as hetero hypnosis. So, it's clear that tradition is wrong. You can obviously be hypnotized without prior training-traditional hypnosis. While early self-hypnosis tends to help later hypnosis.

Therefore, I recommend studying the self-hypnosis procedure and practicing it until you feel comfortable and competent to bring you a relaxed state. Then, use self-therapy for a reasonable amount of time to determine if you are getting the desired results. Only if you get a negative result from such a fair process, you would want to discontinue the technique by yourself or contact an expert? The choice is all yours.

Obviously, "reasonable time" and "fair trial" are not always voluntary and will vary from individual to individual depending on variables such as susceptibility to hypnosis, exercise therapy, level of participation in developmental status, and depth of the problem, or difficulty to deal with the situation.

After setting these variables, I present the following rules of thumb. Even if you faithfully participate in the exercises several times a day for three weeks and give each performance full focus and commitment, there is no indication that you are. If you're not moving toward your goals, you're probably doing something wrong, or your symptoms are rooted in an emotional cause and need professional help to resolve them.

If so, I recommend that you review all aspects of your self-hypnosis to find places where you may not be on the right track. If you still cannot find the answer, seek outside help. If you're a hypnotherapist or feel a more soulful way, you can be a deeper cure expert.

Everything is based on the only principle we can choose. We can choose to be the master of our lives. I'm not talking about the creation of superhumans, but within the bounds of certain reasonable and practical limits, we can get control. I'm sure of that. Perhaps now is the time to take responsibility for a place in your life that can be achieved.

You can assume that each time you exercise, you can trigger your hypnosis faster and more skillfully. Besides, you can add suggestions for appropriate post-hypnotic implants.

"I find my skills in self-hypnosis increasing every day."

Therefore, the progress made by repeating the exercise itself is reinforced by the positive implants intended to reach the unconscious. Performance increases as your skill increases, and confidence increases as your performance increases. One moves the other until you feel more inner strength than you ever felt. You can make it happen. This does not mean that self-hypnosis is a panacea. There is no magic there. It speeds up the results that can be achieved by the more awkward methods of mental and emotional treatment.

The article in this book was clear to gain self-control through self-hypnosis. Before ending, the second important application of hypnosis, the "discovery" practiced in the therapeutic environment, that is, exploring the subconscious to find something hidden in the maze of one's memory. Let me touch on that. It is most useful to reveal important early experiences in our lives through hypnosis. For example, hypnosis highlighted the key memories that led to the successful treatment of Fred. Psychological tests are usually done under the supervision of a second psychotherapist or hypnotherapist. Still, during this time, it is not possible to stop the experiments to unravel the memory of self-hypnosis. Such information can prove valuable in your own self-treatment.

This discovery aspect of hypnosis is increasingly being used to solve puzzles of very practical nature. For example, a person involved in a car crash can hypnotize important details that have been forgotten. Notable is the kidnapping of 26 children on a bus in Chowchilla, California, in 1976. Under hypnosis, the bus driver remembered the kidnapper's license number. This fascinating aspect of hypnosis, the discovery of memory, deserves another opportunity for more extensive research.

At the moment, it's very simple, easy to learn, and powerful, and I'm happy to provide this technique that makes you feel good. It's a good idea to focus on yourself and personalize your controls. Emphasize emotions and feelings with self-hypnosis. Therapists of all beliefs agree with their importance for mental and physical health. So, in a self-hypnosis exercise, imagine a quiet place where you feel peaceful, cherishing your body and mind as kindly as you loved ones, and drawing your spiritual paintings like you. Imagine drawing; want to be-can be. For this reason, it's a good idea to change the wording and images after learning the technique to make it your own.

That is the end of my advice. I can guide you along the way, but you need to do it alone with mental tools and confidence. This is the goal of the analysis. To build the strength of the ego that allows individuals to function productively and happily.

CHAPTER 13: COGNITIVE BEHAVIORAL THERAPY

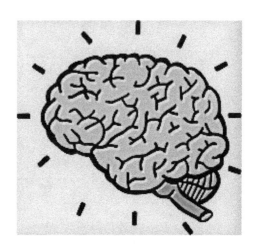

This new form of rehabilitation is known as Cognitive Behavioral Therapy (CBT). It is a widely used treatment used by psychologists around the world to treat obsessive-compulsive disorder, depression, addiction, and a variety of other issues. There is a step by step directions to how to use CBT to bring the brain back into a lean female brain.

There are four basic steps.

1 Learn to distinguish brain hunger (as opposed to physical hunger).

2 Suspending the fancy of two meals.

3 Name and respond to your actual needs.

4 Experience success and measure progress.

Unlike hunger in the brain, physical feelings of hunger have specific objective signs. You will be greeted with a variety of foods to end your stomach humming, low blood sugar, and physical hunger. Brain starvation usually requires very specific foods, and its only physical manifestation, salivation, is usually caused by external events. Step one is the motivation and courage to show two types of hunger. "I have no signs of physical hunger, but I'm hungry for food, I'm hungry."

Step two breaks the fancy of food. To us food is like a polite car salesman who is a friend and only he wants us to buy a car. Learn how to use various cognitive behavioral therapy techniques to redirect firmly fixed thought patterns. We have to recognize what it is and the hallucination of joy for our current wiring. Through mindful practices, you will learn to prove your desire and old belief that eating makes you feel better. In contrast to willpower, this step observes the desire gently but is not forced to react to it.

Step three demonstrates the actual need. Are we tired, stressed, disappointed, angry, or frustrated? We need to take breaks, run, and express disappointment. In other words, you need to meet and address your emotional needs, not your food.

In this step, we continuously recognize success, evaluate progress, and move forward. The human spirit is what we must progress to continue our long journey. The final step in restoring the brain from a food poisoner's brain to a healthy relationship with food depends not only on the level of food addiction but also on the joy you can experience as you progress. The less food addiction, and the more joy we can experience when recognizing progress, the shorter will be the rewiring process. Similarly, the inability to experience acute addiction and the joy of progress slows the rewiring process.

The book does not prescribe diet, but it does show that high flavored and high sugars and salts are addictive. Stopping food addiction means stopping the consumption of these types of foods. The step-by-step program in this book returns your brain to a healthy relationship with food. It does not overwhelm your craving for food. Success does not depend on willpower. Learn how not to allow food to be important in your life and how to regain a healthy perspective.

Cognitive-behavioral therapy was first developed when UCLA psychiatrist Jeffrey M. Schwartz developed it for patients with OCD. CBT is based on the reality that our thoughts provoke emotions, which determine our behavior. To understand the mechanism of CBT, Dr. Schwartz undertook the investigation. Dr. Schwarz's treatment was an obsessive-compulsive hand-wash disorder. Dr. Schwartz first presented a CAT scan of normal brain activity in patients with OCD. Then he showed them photos of his dirty hands. OCD patients are immediately frightened when measured by a brain CAT scan. After observing the CAT scan before and after, and the brain's response to a dirty handheld photograph, the patient was able to change the automated response gradually.

Using a mindful approach, a revolutionary voluntary approach, gradually rewired the brains of OCD patients to see dirty photos on their hands without anxiety. Encouraged by the success of CBT in treating obsessive-compulsive disorder, other medical and psychological experts have begun investigating the use of CBT across obsessive-compulsive disorder. Below is a summary of how CBT was used beyond the initial OCD patients.

Dr. Michael Melzenich, a neurophysiologist at Johns Hopkins, and Dr. Polar Talal, a neuroscientist at the University of Cambridge, work together with children with dyslexia to improve reading accuracy when trained to do the same. It is dramatically improved but distinguishes different sounds. The success of these studies has created "Fast for Word", an organization that has supported more than one million dyslexics in over 40 countries.

Dr. Edward Taub, a behavioral neuroscientist at Columbia University, has extended the

CBT protocol to develop obsessive-compulsive exercise therapy. This has led to significant advances in helping thousands of patients recover from stroke-related nerve damage.

Another UCLA neuroscientist, Dr. John Piacentini, has documented the efficacy of CBT in Tourette's syndrome. Dr. Piacentini's CBT protocol includes tic recognition training. It teaches Tourette patients how to monitor themselves for early signs of imminent tics. Training with competing reactions teaches patients how to engage in spontaneous behavior designed to be physically incompatible with the next tic, interrupting cycles and reducing tics.

Dr. John D. Teesdale, a researcher at Oxford and Cambridge, created a unique CBT protocol for clinically depressed patients based on a multilevel theory of mind called Interacting Cognitive Subsystems (ICS). The

ICS model explains that the mind has several modes of receiving and processing new information, cognitively and emotionally. This theory links a person's susceptibility to depression with trust in only one of the available modes and falsely blocks all other options. Prevention of recurrence of depression is based on the individual's ability to easily move between the many modes available, away from the black and white thought modes.

Initially, it was difficult to get the scientific elite to believe that people could alter the workings of the brain by focusing their attention in another way. This process did not include not only self-initiated neuroplasticity but also effective drugs that change the mind and comprehensive psychoanalytic counseling. With so much success, CBT is internationally favored as a practical tool for overcoming psychological and physical conditions that overcome long-term disability. This positive and practical remedy is popular with both therapists and patients. It is to restore the natural neural network that changes our attitude towards our impulses in this case about food.

Yes, our addicts had flaws in their brain wiring that caused overwhelming cravings and forced us into slavery when we were not physically hungry. However, what CBT offers is the ability to use the activity in an existing healthy circuit using mental focus. George Guilder, the author of Microcosm and Telecosm, nominates the doctor Schwartz's CBT "Bold rescue of the Free Will Concept."

In this chapter, we will first look for how the brain of a thin woman works, and then we will compare it to the will powered thin woman. Then we will finally explore how the use of cognitive-behavioral theory while practicing mindfulness can help to lose weight without going through emotional suppression and stress.

NATURAL THINNESS

I would like to make an important distinction between naturally lean women, and will powered lean women, with willpower, self-denial, and strict routines. What I have found is that there are striking differences between women of both types. A thin woman has a healthy relationship with food, in contrast to the fat woman, who is trying to lose fat by forced calorie counting, excessive exercise, and life focused on her profession, to stay thin at all costs. I know her strategy very well and have seen people continue using the same fanatic methods to reach the thinness for many periods.

Small dishes, strict nutrition, counting all calories, drinking a lot of water, and all the tools used by lean women with a strong will are useful and can be used as useful starting points. However, this book is not intended to increase your diving board. Check out at the supermarket, and you'll find many of them in most women's magazines. We're presenting a way to go beyond crutches because if you throw them away before a meaningful cure, your injury will recover. Weight loss is temporary and will be avoided if it is based on the use of aids. The thinness of nature is not a function of willpower. Willpower is limited and exhausted by many of our external demands and our emotional challenges. And a functional crutch should be thrown away when its purpose is achieved.

The central nervous system (including the brain and spinal cord) is formed of two basic types of cells, neurons and glia. Neurons are messengers of information. They are structures that exchange chemicals that emit electrical impulses that send signals not only between different regions of the brain but also between the brain and the rest of the nervous system. Everything we think and feel begins with the brain, correlates with the neural activity that affects other parts of our body, and is reflected in nerve cells in the spinal cord. As we humans learn new skills, the wiring of our brain becomes more complex and interrelated.

As a person who has been witnessing people overeating for years and years, I know there are quite a few neural circuits that support these behaviors. One way to think of the neural network of overeating is that it is part of an organic program that sends electrical and chemical signals whenever emotional, situational, or social stress causes hunger. What we have learned in our program is that we can equally restore the neural networks that recognize hunger in the brain and, in some practice, empower them. programming. Therefore, our goal is to restore a neural network of naturally lean women.

Changes are biological and can be measured at the brain level and CAT scan and MRI. It is to restore the behavior of the naturally lean women, including the ability to experience satisfaction in a luxurious feast. It's not a coping tool that calls your friends or, in our case, runs to the fridge each time you face a stressful challenge. It's also not emotional. It doesn't survive the longing for another. Many of us experienced an early stage of love that resisted the fascinating things in your life. This is exactly the process that is happening in the brains of lean women with a strong will, overwhelmed by power-the need for overeating overpower the desire to stay lean. Many of us can maintain this inhibitory mechanism, but only if we have enough emotional energy to overwhelm our insatiable appetite.

I have lived in the Will powered thin woman administration. And, like most women, I'm sure they'll resort to overeating as soon as they don't get a small plate or their lover is gone. In this book, we will restore the neural network of a naturally lean woman by rewiring the brain and selecting behaviors that lead to a healthy relationship with food. This is not an act of will or intellectual structure. It's a sensation triggered by organic brain structures, and the naturally lean female neural network does not equate overeating with pleasure.

The goal is to move from a conceptual brain understanding of the sacred. If at the moment, we recognize the joy of eating and have the ability to recognize it without the overwhelming urge to enjoy it. At the biological level, naturally, lean women have different structure of the body. It is organic and natural, and through negotiations about inner conflicts and what to eat, it leads to the confidence and brain signals without the stress experienced by an unmotivated lean woman. The wiring of naturally thin exhibits wisdom and, at the same time, allows you to accept the potential pleasure of eating and consciously choose to lose or delay that pleasure until you are gradually hungry.

Be clear about women who eat like a naturally thin woman and women who eat like will powered thin woman. There are physiological differences between the brains of both types of women, those who are naturally thin, and those who are working hard to lose weight. Thinning at the expense of high stress and will is a recipe we've all tried and has failed many times. There are healthy and workable ways to lose weight all at once. One of these ways is practicing the mindfulness through which cognitive behavioral modification is administered in everyday lifestyle, leading to normal weight maintenance without stress and anxiety.

MINDFULNESS

The most important skills needed to administer cognitive behavioral therapy is the ability to be mindful.

Modern women usually do not currently exist in the present. Usually, she looks at past events and predicts the future. Mindfulness sometimes means accepting and maintaining a curiosity about our thoughts, feelings, physical sensations, and perceptions of the environment. It may sound useless. But learning to experience the present moment in a way that abolishes judgment and self-criticism has an incredibly good impact on our biology, happiness, and ability to maintain equality of events that normally lead to overeating. This gives you a broader perspective and gives you additional options and clarity when making decisions.

It's not just about paying attention to teachers 'lectures and friends' conversations. It's a "meta-consciousness," and it notices where your attention is directed. So, if you're paying attention during a lecture, you know you're paying attention. While driving, paying attention not only to focus on the road, but also to the movement of the hand that holds the steering wheel, the movement of the neck when checking traffic conditions, and the grunts under the road. Mindfulness is the ability to pay attention intentionally.

Mindfulness also requires acceptance. That means not believing that there are "right" or "wrong" ways of thinking and feelings at a particular moment, and paying attention to your thoughts and feelings without judging them. When practicing mindfulness, our thinking is in harmony with what we feel in the present moment, rather than warming the past or imagining the future.

At any time, focus on the myriad aspects of your current experience. For example, suppose you had dinner, and your child immediately said, "I hate chicken!" You pay attention to your body's reactions, the anger, and frustration that develops. When I notice the racing pulse, the idea of "I worked hard on this dinner after a long day..." comes to mind. Not only do you realize you are experiencing anger, but you accept anger and accept something without judgment. The next paragraph describes how Jon Kabat-Zinn, one of the leading mindfulness teachers, described his progress.

"When I started practicing mindfulness, I thought at every moment to see how amazing everything was. One of the books I read was dishwashing, water, soap. When I tried it, the inner monologue said, "Oh, the water was very warm, this soap has a very nice scent and is very relaxing." A delusion is felt that was strange, strange, and light. Getting mindful attention means knowing and accepting what it is. Perceive the sensation without assigning a positive or negative value. You only notice that there is water in your hand or the scent of soap. Do not notice and judge. This is not a creepy story. Because this is where the left side of the brain penetrates. It's about being aware of our thinking and responding to challenges in a balanced way."

Bringing this kind of mindful consciousness to hunger should be relatively emotional, so it's a relatively easy way to start practicing. And as it learns new skills to pay attention to the small cases of hunger in the brain, it helps combat the overwhelming desire to overeat when it occurs. By witnessing, we begin to weaken excessive eating habits and eliminate subconscious reactions. I also arrest negative soliloquy that comes to my mind.

Most people find it helpful to know that mindfulness practices produce very high returns. A simple analogy is physical muscle development. When heavier, it modifies the body's tissues in two ways:

• Increase in basic strength.

• Increase in basic flexibility.

When investing in mindfulness practice, try formal procedures (such as meditation) that alter the organization of consciousness in two ways.

• Making the baseline clearer.

• Increasing basic rewards.

The purpose of strength training is not to achieve a temporary state of strength and flexibility that exists when you exercise and then disappears throughout the day. The goal is to increase your strength and flexibility gradually. In other words, the purpose is to acquire the permanent properties of your body.

Similarly, the goal of mindfulness practice is not to achieve the temporary state of clarity and serenity that exists when you meditate and then disappear all day. The goal of mindfulness practice is to elicit the desire for overeating but gradually improve the clarity and develop equality for observing overeating without forcing a response. It is not to develop an intellectual understanding of excessive feeding activity, but to cultivate a calm, reliable balance and confidence to respond to excessive food triggers that are conscious and impulsive and respond without fear and force.

The sooner we can experience equality, the sooner we can start using the Falls of Mindfulness Practice.

PROPER PLANNING

The better this program helps you to recover your healthy brain at a time, and once you are ready to return to a healthy weight, the more likely you are to succeed.

You need to spend time on activities that promote you and improve your quality of life. Scientists are recording the power of positive thinking. By utilizing the force of the positive posture, the time required to restore the NATURALLY THIN WOMAN'S neural network can be greatly reduced.

Resilience and tenacity are important during this transition home. Self-sympathy also contributes to success.

One of the last tips I suggest is a serious commitment to stress-free your brain. Most of today's stress comes from our thoughts, not from the outside world. In other words, you can manage your stress by changing your mind. Investing in a healthy reseller for what really costs you will improve the overall quality of your work and life. Remember, that is a process. Through strategies such as meditation and frequent mindful moments, you can achieve the equality needed for a successful, NATURALLY THIN WOMAN program. And don't forget to get acquainted with what works for you. What worked for me may not work the same for you. This is what our topic was designed to overcome bumps on the road. This is not a single program. It is a program aimed at adjusting to your health and the meaning of nature to you, not to other societies.

CHAPTER 14: LEVERAGING COGNITIVE BEHAVIORAL THERAPY

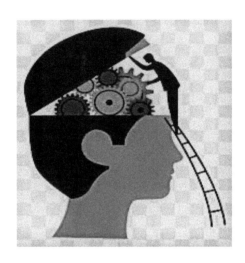

The question after I learned about CBT was simple. These types of treatments can be used to rewire the brains obsessed with the food. But do you mostly adopt the behavior of lean women naturally? The answer was yes!

Needless to say, if we can eliminate food obsession, obsessive eating, and pointless overeating, we can free ourselves from the diet tyranny. Rewiring the brain to have a healthy relationship with food has nothing to do with obsessive or modest self-discipline. It's not even a dreadful watch that allows so many women to lose weight but feel stressed. Instead, we naturally regain a thin behavior as a normal dietary response.

Because the brain can change (neuroplasticity), the process of consciously repeating mindfulness changes the brain's neural circuits at the physical level. A measure for achieving the behavior of naturally lean women is that food does not create an internal struggle that appears to require willpower. We have already mentioned the various behaviors characteristic of naturally lean women. Let's take a closer look at one of these major actions, especially eating on an empty stomach.

To understand what is physical hunger, let's first look at what is happening in the body:

When our bodies burn food in our stomachs, and our blood sugar and insulin levels begin to fall, the cells that line our stomachs produce a hormone called ghrelin. Ghrelin communicates with the hypothalamus, deep in the brain. The hypothalamus regulates basic physical functions such as hunger, thirst, sleep, and libido. As soon as the hypothalamus receives a message from ghrelin that it needs to eat something to keep moving, it triggers the release of our appetite-stimulating neuropeptide.

My God! I'm starting to get hungry.

The specific signs of physical hunger are:

Your blood sugar level is low, and you may feel nauseous. The taste of the tongue awakens completely, and you welcome any kind of food. You do not want a specific meal.

The problem is how your brain reacts when you look at food. Overeating leads to a desire to eat, often in response to visual cues, when you are not physically hungry. This is known as "external food hypersensitivity," and also known as EFS. Food addicts also respond to "situational starvation." Let's see what hunger means:

Social. We hope to connect us with others and want to eat to share shared experiences. We also tend to dine in social situations to avoid inappropriate feelings or because the party is uncommitted.

Sensual. Eat because there is food at the restaurant, see ads for a specific meal, or pass by a fragrant bakery. The desire to eat reacts because it is closely linked to a particular activity (watching TV, going to a movie, attending a sporting event, etc.).

Thought. Eating as a result of negative self-talk or as an excuse for a meal. The irony is that if you scold yourself for lack of willpower, it can be triggered.

Physiological. Eating in response to physical ailments such as headaches and other pain.

Emotional. Eating in response to stress, boredom, fatigue, tension, anger, fear, and loneliness. Instead of effectively dealing with the underlying emotions, eating suppresses emotions and shifts the focus to what seems initially to be a joy. Unfortunately, we indulge in a reminder after eating.

You can learn how to keep an eye on the fear of starvation in context. The Thin Cognitive Behavioral Protocol (see TCB) consists of four basic steps.

Step 1: Recognize brain hunger.

Step 2: Break obsessive food thinking.

Step 3: Name and address your actual needs.

Step 4: Measure your progress and experience success. The goal is to perform these steps for 21-42 consecutive days until the rewiring is deeply rooted. The first three steps are important, especially at the beginning of the process.

STEP 1: RECOGNIZE BRAIN HUNGER

When it comes to overeating, there are many situations and emotional imbalances that cause obsessive feeding fantasies and the need for forced feeding. Craving for food has a real physiological effect on our bodies. Water begins to come out of our mouth. It's exciting to expect the fun of eating. This can be measured as an increase in brain activity. Your heart rate will increase, and your anxiety level will increase. I want to experience this fun. The brain releases neurochemicals, lowering blood sugar levels in anticipation of the next sugar. This is why we feel unstable and moody when we have brain hunger.

An important first step is the ability to recognize brain hunger. This is not achieved by superficial, occasional observations. Rather, we consciously recognize that "hunger," which feels very compelling, is not physical, but an obsession. Useful help is to check for signs of physical hunger when taking a deep breath. The other is to ask yourself when you were full or when you were feeling full at the end. This process allows us to be proactive in: This is hunger, and this desire is an obsession. "The goal of Step 1 is to figure out if the need arising is a misfire in the brain." The brain has a biochemical imbalance. Wired to experience an imbalance. This desire is a misfire in the brain."

It does not resist the urge to overeat. We are already using a lot of willpower to stick to our diet. Instead, it recognizes and names the hunger for what it is, without rattling our brains or causing additional fear. Learning to calmly and unambiguously name the hunger of the brain enhances our ability to observe it without devoting it to something to eat. The willingness to accept that hunger is not physical is a huge step forward. Acknowledgments stop the forced and automatic reaction to hunger in some situations. It changes impulses. However, recognizing situational hunger without performing steps 2 and 3 does not eliminate hunger.

Trying to call hunger "situational" or "emotional" scares us, but we continue to invest in tools that improve our ability to perform Step 1, especially in the practice of mindfulness.

STEP 2: BREAK OBSESSIVE FOOD THINKING

The ability to interfere with the idea of obsessive eating was examined by Dr. Suzanne Segerstrom of the University of Kentucky. She assumed the theory she called "pausing and planning." Dr. Segerstrom documents that what we experience as an internal conflict is the ability to pause or slow down and weigh the effects of "I want to experience this joy" and "I do not want to." This personal ability determines the ability to perform this interrupt step.

If you can stop the automated reaction to eating, there is usually emotional conflict. Let's see what gets activated in our brain when we experience the struggle of "I want to" and "I don't want to." As explained earlier in the previous chapter, there are many chemical changes in our brain that we overeat. A chronic diet rewired our brain and experienced a hungry brain without food shortages. Biologically, you have the opportunity to enjoy food even if you are not hungry. Finally, we have formed strong bonds between some foods that meet some of our emotional needs-comfort, excitement, relaxation, love, to name a few. The brain has deep structures called the caudate nucleus. Scientists around the world are studying this structure and believe that the caudate may not function properly in people with obsessive-compulsive behavior. Think of the caudate as a processing center for body movements, physical emotions, learning, and planning. The Caudate core, together with its sister structure Putamen, functions like an automatic transmission in a car. These guarantee a smooth transition from one behavior to another.

During a normal day, we make lots of fast, smooth, easy, thoughtless, and quick behavior changes. It is the caudate and putamen that make this possible. The problem with obsessive-compulsive people is that the smooth transition of thoughts and actions is disturbed by disturbances of the caudal nucleus. As a result of this dysfunction, the front part of the brain becomes overactive and consumes excess energy. It looks like your car is stuck in a ditch. You spin the wheel, but you can't get out of the trench until you manually shift gears to get traction. If a brute force bin feels "I'm hungry," and it doesn't go away, it's the same as spinning our tires. It is necessary to carefully investigate what triggers situational hunger by switching from automation to manual mode and unknowingly accepting

"I'm hungry." If you succumb to brain hunger, you will feel temporary relief. The technical term for this is the "suction effect." But in a very short time, the urge increases and sometimes walks its own life, becoming a full-fledged binge!

STEP 3: NAME AND ADDRESS YOUR ACTUAL NEEDS

The most difficult task is following this step. Our brain is always running programs like computers. We are aware of some of them. Some of them are completely unconscious. Many of these programs are so deep-rooted that they have an involuntary response as well as a knee-like response when hit with a rubber mallet. The important point to be aware of is that due to the current wiring, various unconscious programs lead to overeating.

By naming and addressing needs, we stop overeating and instead direct energy to what is currently disguised as hungry. Part of the hunger reaction is due to situational triggers and another part of the chronic suppression of our basic emotional needs. If naming is difficult, you may need self-advocacy coaching or help with history to help control the root cause. Are you stressed about work, money problems, difficulties with loved ones? Do you just want to fit unconsciously in a social situation where everyone else is eating? By naming hidden needs, we can approach our processes so that our emotions are not kidnapped and address our real needs rather than overeating.

As a result, repeating steps 1 to 3 alters the biochemistry of the brain, causing atrophy of the neural network that causes contextual hunger.

STEP 4: MEASURE YOUR PROGRESS AND EXPERIENCE SUCCESS

Neuroplasticity is the ability to change our own brain, occurs when we quietly observe the hunger of our brain and are not afraid. This does not happen overnight. Like strength training, it requires repetition, which leads to healthy structure and creates habits. This strengthens the connections between neural networks (brain cells) and increases the likelihood that they will fire together in the future. Neural networks, the cells that carry information in the brain, essentially reinforce the affinity between neurons by reorganizing their electrochemical relationships. The neuroscientist mantra is "the cells that fire together wires up."

Upon success, dopamine will be given. If we are happy with our progress, this shows that the naturally lean female neural network is self-healing and rewiring. The more involved in the behavior of naturally lean women, the more likely it is that some satisfaction will be created. Keep in mind that when you reach your goal, dopamine is also created. If we fail, it means that the behavior of a naturally lean woman has not been captured.

In the field of the computer industry, the importance of progress is often documented. Among the well-known publication Computer-Human Interface Percentage Progress Indicators, Dr. Brad A. Myers of the University of Toronto says that he prefers progress indicators when waiting for a task to complete. Software development teams whose goals are shared in the short term and whose progress is visible are 90% more likely to complete their projects successfully than teams whose progress is tracked loosely and not shared. In her book Rules of Play, Katie Salen (Ph.D.) from New School for Design and Eric Zimmerman (MIT) from MIT, unless participants have a meaningful tool to measure progress, we have concluded that consistent engagement is unlikely.

Naturally, I am satisfied with achieving my goals, even if they are mini-goals. This advancement increases satisfaction and increases the likelihood of continuing the rewiring process. "When we completed a complex task, we found that the brain released a large number of endorphins."

Tracking progress plays an important role in rewiring because it affects the ability to find, complete, and comply with the Thin Cognitive Behavior (TCB) protocol. There is no motivation without progress. What has proven to be effective is certain persecution in a way that is important to you.

An image on the front of the refrigerator that shows weekly progress as a number and / or image and / or graph.

Measuring and experiencing the progress during the reroute will make the reroute much more likely. If you're not motivated, you'll never finish rewiring, because nothing prevents you from reaching your next goal, your next improvement. If you don't recognize your progress, you are more likely to give up. Without motivation, there is no progress. It won't end without progress!

"It's often said that motivation doesn't last. Well, neither does bathing, and so we recommend it every day."

Jig Ziggler, Motivational Writer, Speaker.

Step 4 evaluates the effectiveness of the TCB process. Here we measure whether or not the repetition is rewarded. If you suffer from brain hunger, compare this present situational hunger event with its last occurrence. Ask yourself:

Since you have identified hunger as a situation, can you identify the root cause of the misfire? Can you effectively deal with the underlying trigger? That is, how easy and difficult were steps 1 to 3 this time? Are they effortless, natural, fluent, and free of trauma?

The psychological view of progress inevitably shapes and inspires our efforts. In this step, "Experience Success," you will evaluate your progress. It's important to track progress so that everyone can complete the rewiring process. Without indicators, progress cannot be measured. Without measuring progress, the chances of success are low. I am preparing for failure.

The following scale shows my commitment to the rewiring process. This type of scale is important for tracking your progress. In human psychology, we are most likely to give up if we do not experience progress. How a mental process progresses is emotionally different when compared to stagnation. Progress contributes to endurance and builds confidence.

Use the table below if it helps. If it doesn't help, create it yourself.

Difficulty = Emotional experience.

10 = Willingness with white knuckles, stratospheric fear, the tremendous concentration required.

9 = Intense concentration required, extreme fear.

8 = High fear level, difficult concentration still required.

7 = Challenge to fear, Concentration still needed.

6 = Fear level is still increasing, and caution is still needed.

5 = Fear level is still above normal but manageable.

4 = Some fear. However, I'm sure the steps are complete.

3 = Fear is low.

 2 = recognition of fear.

1 = Zero fight.

DON'T BE AFRAID

Due to several issues and the complexity of status triggers, the "measuring progress" in this step is probably not evenly evaluated for each trigger. For example, progress may be easier to understand when you need a break than when you feel an inappropriate feeling.

After using the TCB protocol, I found that my "morning hunger" was caused by my inability to recognize physical limitations. Within a week of the start of the protocol, this type of need for food quickly recognized the need for a break, as the intensity of the "requires a snack" dropped significantly. I was able to change gears, go for a walk, and get back to work without a snack. When I measured my progress in the morning snack area, it went from 9 (requires effort) to 2 (awareness of anxiety).

On the other hand, dealing with loved ones, especially those with a long history of conflict, is like spinning a wheel in the mud, and I have measured zero progress. I was just frustrated and ran in the fridge. I kept trying to use the TCB protocol but couldn't go through step 1 (I know I'm was physically hungry). After realizing that I was stuck, I finally admitted that I needed help in this area.

One of my friends suggested listening positively. It's a communication skill developed by Carl Rogers. This process requires that one person speak and reflect on what they hear before the second person speaks. This exchange is repeated until both people feel what they hear. After using the active hearing process, it took a month before the effort was significantly reduced. It was gradual but eventually reached a low number. I haven't solved all the differences with this person, but now I can interact with them without overeating.

Note that the first type of situation (which requires a break) starvation was to meet personal needs. However, the second type (competition) involves interacting with others. The second type required additional resources (in the form of communication tools) before being comfortable.

For this reason, it is important to distinguish between significant progress and challenges. Little or no progress, this usually means an area where external assistance is needed. Return to an automatic analogy: In most cases, a manual switch will help you get out of the mud. However, if the mud is deep and slippery, you may need a tow truck.

CHAPTER 15: HOW TO START MINDFUL EATING

You certainly already know: Naturally lean women have several properties that lead to a healthy relationship with food:

1. They only eat when they are physically hungry.

2. They take time to prepare a healthy meal.

3. They focus on their eating experience and, if possible, eat them silently.

4. If possible, they eat in a nice place.

5. They enjoy the food.

6. They only take a small bite.

7. They often put the dishes down.

8. They slowly and completely chew the food.

9. They breathe consciously before chewing the food.

10. If food loses its taste, they stop eating immediately.

What is the basis of most of these habits? Eat wholeheartedly. I was always intrigued when Naturally Thin Women used this phrase. But what is mindful eating? I wanted to know what they did when they ate carefully. Use four TCB steps to restore these 10 NATURALLY THIN WOMEN'S properties. Let's check them out:

1: Recognize old patterns step

2: interrupt the old pattern step

3: Perform NTW operation steps mindfully and with complete attention

4: Measure progress and experience success

Now we will go through all these properties of naturally thin women in a detailed manner:

RECOGNIZING PHYSICAL HUNGER

STEP 1: IDENTIFY STARVATION FOR THE SITUATION

Five types of triggers instigate current overeating programming. All of them are explained below:

Social Incentives: They eat to avoid feelings of inadequacy or to share a common experience, hoping that it connects them to the others. There is scientific evidence that we eat quite a lot when we eat in a social environment.

Sensual Trigger: Eat for Opportunity, Eat Donuts at Work, Advertise Food for Food on TV, or Pass by the Bakery. I didn't feel the need to nourish my body, but I had the opportunity to experience joy and suddenly felt hungry. In these cases, the desire to eat is an opportunity to experience the learned reaction, a pleasure to external triggers. We weren't hungry until we saw the visual food.

The motivation for thought: Eating as a result of internal dialogue that condemns oneself. We offend ourselves, and ironically, succumbing to overeating usually reprimands us for lack of willpower.

Physiological trigger: Eating in response to a physical effect (e.g., headache or other pain).

Emotional triggers: Eating in response to boredom, stress, fatigue, tension, depression, anger, fear, and loneliness. These triggers are as simple as a lack of cognition in the body (I need a physical break) or as complex as suppressed emotions (I'm a member of a toxic family).

STEP 2: BREAK THE OBSESSION

My brain is crazy about food. I'm hungry and wired to make me feel obsessive about responding to food. This is my current wiring that uses food depending on different situational triggers.

STEP 3: NAME AND ADDRESS YOUR ACTUAL NEEDS

Depending on the situation, you have the option of how to respond effectively to the trigger.

Social Trigger: To fulfill the desire to connect with others, I can try a few small bites and rave about the food. Even better, you can start an exciting conversation about something other than food.

TCB Answer: This is not a pang of physical hunger. This is my desire to adapt to society.

Sensual Trigger: Recognizing my usual reaction to the visual appeal of food. I admit I wasn't hungry before I saw the food. We must admit that this is not physical hunger; it is an automated response to the unexpected.

TCB Answer: This is not a pang of physical hunger. This is my Pavlov's response to a highly charged stimulus. I want to enjoy the pleasure that food presents. If I eat this sweet, I will feel better.

Motivation: Recognizing the usual reaction to negative thoughts, pain, and discomfort.

Ending emotional stress is a normal human reaction. I have alternative and meaningful ways to deal with feelings of inadequacy.

TCB Answer: This is not a pang of physical hunger. Eating is a way for me to calm down and how I weaken my painful thoughts. I have the tools or can get the help I need to deal with the painful dialogue inside.

Physiological triggers: There are more effective tools (medication as needed) to deal with physical complaints.

TCB Answer: This is not a pang of physical hunger. This is a learned response to physical illness.

Emotional triggers: You can identify what triggers your emotional hunger and choose to act effectively.

TCB Answer: This is not physical hunger. That is my standard coping mechanism and current wiring.

STEP 4: MEASURE PROGRESS

What about after performing steps 1-3? The scales in the Step 4-Measures of Progress and Experience of Success section help you measure progress as you adopt individual characteristics. The more you practice, the easier it will be.

Is possible for you to respond to each signal in an appropriate manner? If the answer is no, what is your stress level? Need to reduce stress first? What are the wise decisions to meet your actual needs?

TAKE TIME TO PREPARE A HEALTHY MEAL

Home cooking has many advantages because it's a form of mindfulness. You personally choose high quality and nutritious ingredients. Keep in mind that grocery stores are based on cheap fats and cheap carbohydrates, not your nutritional value. You are controlling where your calories come from: they come from trans fats, additional sugars, well! They ensure that there are no flavor enhancers like MSG or other brain-disrupting substances. As mentioned earlier, the net effect of these addictive substances is that you eat more. Creating a healthy diet is expressing your love for yourself and your family. It's a creative achievement. Save money with this exciting vacation-like activity in Tahiti, Paris, and the Galapagos Islands. You can spend as much time as you want. You can come up with several tricks and shortcuts to save time in the kitchen. It is honest and to recover your cooking skills. It only takes a few hours to revive the master chef inside. While to go somewhere to pick up food. Clarify the facts, go there, park, get food, eat there, or take it home. According to the Center for Disease Control (CDC), cases of more than 76,000,000 people who suffered from food poisoning annually due to bacteria, viruses, and parasites that lead to food contamination.

Think about it; you have to eat carefully. The only area that affects 95% of this possibility is the quality of the food you eat. If you don't know who cooks or exactly what ingredients they use, are they cheap trans-fat oils, lots of extra sodium, extra sugar? How can you manage yourself?

SITTING IN BEAUTY

Establish a simple and beautiful environment, especially if you eat alone. Even if you're hungry, it can take a few minutes to reach an attractive setting. If you don't have the time, are in a hurry, and want to eat directly from the fridge, this is a big sign that you're usually absorbed in foods that are perceived as high levels of anxiety. This may feel irresistible while restoring a naturally lean female neural network. This heals the "hungry brain," so it is important to calm before eating. There are several ways to reduce high levels of anxiety. Deep breathing, meditation, journaling, active jogging, and anything else that seems personally effective in reaching a place of peace. Remember to measure your progress. Can you set up the table without fear? If not, could you be wise to identify the cause of anxiety and address it?

EATING EXPERIENCE

In a culture that emphasizes multitasking, eating is a secondary activity. We do not combine food with the nutrition of our bodies. Eating is what we do without attention while doing more meaningful work.

Have you automatically turned off your car radio while looking for a new address? I instinctively know that removing a voice stimulus increases your ability to focus on finding its address. Silence also allows us to pay attention only to food and to be fully present for a dining experience. Watching TV, interacting with computers, talking on the phone, reading books, and doing other activities is not a supplement to a careful diet. Mindful meals require indiscriminate attention, so it's a great way to overeat.

If you have resistance to silent hoods, rewiring can help you recognize that you ate for the first time when you had another activity. It is a custom that has been cultivated for many years. You rarely eat the main focus.

When you sit quietly and eat, you can hear inner conversations such as how to enjoy the meal and subtle messages from the body when you are satisfied. If turning off competing stimuli creates fear, inhale, and note the cause of the anxiety.

If you are dining with your family, invite them to participate in the careful process of eating. Trying to turn off as many distractions as you can during your meal is better than overeating during multitasking. Discuss your senses and taste of food. Slow food does not have to be extreme. Nevertheless, it is a good idea to remind the family that eating is not a race. Encourage the family to chew on every slice of food, examining the taste, texture, and odor in detail. Ask them about their feelings, thank them for collecting brownie points, and thank them for their blessings and share their meals with their families.

Remember to measure your progress: how do you feel in silence after a meal? Can you eliminate all distractions and eat quietly without fear? Is practicing this property easier to eat silently?

ENJOY YOUR MEAL

Of course, the thin women have an internal dialogue of appreciation and appreciation and joy: "This is delicious. And it saturates. Shoveling food not only misses every bite of taste, but the entertainment center is in place. You'll need more food to meet gourmet merchants because you're not inspired by it.

We acknowledge that this resistance to internal dialogue is the current practice of not attending for the pleasure of eating. Usually, our conversation feeds on something other than our body, so it's more relevant to issues, concerns, and current to-do lists.

If you pay 100% attention to eating and enjoy eating carefully, you will find that the restoration of NATURALLY THIN WOMEN'S wiring is approaching.

Remember to measure your progress. How do you feel after allowing an internal dialogue about the pleasure of eating? Do you enjoy this conversation without fear? If the answer is no, what are the obstacles to achieving this trait?

SMALL BITES

If you overeat food, you will burn more calories and experience the same amount of pleasure. We must recognize that we have made significant efforts in the past. The wise action is to eat some meals with a small spoon like a wheel while we learn to take smaller bites. However, once you measure progress in this area, it is essential to make the scoop larger. The reason is that if you take a small bite just because the spoon is low, the neural network won't be restored, and you are entirely dependent on the tool.

Don't forget to check for your progress. How does it feel like after eating the whole meal with just a few bites? How was your fear? Did you experience the fun with such a small morsel? Did you have to hit the kitchen and get a more oversized spoon? Or did you just start eating with your fingers?

FORK DOWN

Whatever your fork or tableware is placed in a bite, you are encouraged to eat wholeheartedly. We are ready to enjoy every bite, every bite, every subtlety, every spice, every texture. Eating is foreplay, not a race. It's a sensual experience. Arashi defeats the purpose.

Remember to measure your progress: how do you feel after eating a complete meal and placing a fork in a bite? What is your fear level? Would you like to enjoy the delicacy of food?

CHEW SLOWLY AND THOROUGHLY

For many obsessive eaters, diet represents a solution for drug users. The faster you can move the shovel, the quicker you can get up. Unfortunately, this behavior leads to total calorie burn and shortens the sensation of pleasure. We try to raise our dopamine levels as soon as possible! We've been doing this for a long time, so biting slowly and slowly can be anxious.

The digestion begins with the first bite, causes the release of saliva, disinfects food, and smooths the way to the stomach. As we bit, the brain releases neurotransmitters that tell the hypothalamus that we are full. Wholly and slowly chewing will remove even the slightest aroma and increase your enjoyment.

Remember to measure your progress. How do you feel after biting slowly? What was your fear? Can you enjoy the slowdown without fear?

BREATHING

After swallowing, breathing three times will reconnect with the body. If you prefer, it is a kind of palate wash. Readjust for the next bite sensual experience. This is also an opportunity to help us determine if we are full.

Remember to measure your progress. Do you breathe three times during one bite with one meal? Did you notice that your anxiety is growing? Did you enjoy your meal?

EXPERIENCE FULLNESS

If you eat it carefully, you'll be full if you lose the taste! By contrast, they are looking for salt, ketchup, mayo, mustard, sugar, or barbecue sauces as overeaters. It's something you can regain a comfortable experience and "enjoy" your food. Additives are an attempt to nullify the intelligence that tells you that you have enough.

I've certainly heard the advice to wait 20 minutes for your brain to catch up with your ecstasy. But when we eat at piranha speed, we consume a lot of food. We don't know how to wait. Until then, everything was invisible. Besides, our brain isn't too slow! By paying attention to when food loses its initial appeal, we can instantly know when it is full.

Note that the beginning of this process feels strange. After all, we are used to consuming everything on the plate. For many of us, throwing away food is very difficult because our conditioning to eat everything on the plate is rooted. A useful tool is to visualize excess food as fat in your favorite body parts. Your taste will tell him that he is good enough, and all overconsumption turns into fat.

Also, understand that we are accustomed to stomach congestion and no food consumption. Initially, this is done mechanically, but if you repeat this a few times, you get the actual saturation. Besides, regaining confidence in the palate signal feels free, as you no longer need to experience the severity of a clogged sensation after a meal. The energy satisfaction after eating, rather than lethargy or immobility, regains your sense of freedom.

Remember to measure your progress. Can you say "it was great" and "I'm full" without having to stuff myself? Can you recognize the abundance?

CHAPTER 16: TOOLS FOR THIN COGNITIVE BEHAVIOR

In this chapter, we will discuss useful tools for thin cognitive behavior. We will do it for each step, so first let's review what these steps are:

1. Recognizing brain hunger
2. Interrupting obsessive food thoughts
3. Naming and addressing the real need

TOOLS FOR RECOGNIZING BRAIN HUNGER

Detecting brain hunger is the key to the rewiring process. We try to restore this ability when our anxiety level is in the stratosphere, or when we feel the pressure to participate in social ceremonies, or when we do not have access to masquerades where hunger exacerbates the problem. Mindfulness practices give us equality to physically recognize the body, more easily accept emotions, and protect ourselves from the unhealthy response to social pressures. If we're careful, instead of cutting off the overwhelming wiring depicted as desire (due to uncomfortable social circumstances, peer pressure, or inadequate emotions) and spending powerlessly, you can engage in alternative practices.

Meditation is most commonly referred to as a means of achieving mindfulness and thereby recognizing brain hunger. If the idea of meditation is actively provoking you (and this is understandable for today's modern-day women), try some form of active meditation (such as swimming).

Here are other helpful tips for achieving mindfulness without meditation:

For example, decide whether to return to mindfulness several times during a busy day, move slowly in your life, or be overly aware of your surroundings. An example of how you can become over conscious is to recognize something new every day as you walk through the park you want to walk.

The decisive factor is to be careful, and it just doesn't happen. By developing a Mindful Trigger as described in this chapter, you can remind yourself to lead a conscious life. Remember, we have to be aware of the hunger of the brain, and we need to be aware of physical hunger. The success of repeating TCB steps accelerates and strengthens rewiring! These neural networks are restored when a food panic occurs and can calmly observe what is called brain hunger, and identify emotional needs that need to be addressed. This is an experience where you don't have to worry about it, and you don't overeat.

MINDFULNESS AIDS

Following are some tips that will be helpful to obtain mindfulness:

- **Laugh in Public**-Laughing not only makes you feel better, but it also creates a positive energy exchange when you interact with someone. Name the mood-Running the same activity in different moods will produce different·results. Note how mood affects biology? Reconnect with Your Body-Be aware of your body position and how it affects you. Is your body nervous or open and fluid?

- **Return to yourself before being with someone**-Breathe and return to yourself before interacting directly with someone by phone or email. When the phone rings, you need to be careful again. The caller makes you fresh, present, and available.

- **Something old or new-**become aware of something new when you are walking down a frequent path. There can be multiple things you can pay attention to, such as computer keystrokes, birds' chirping, the gentle roar of an airplane above you, or Your footsteps or many more.

- **Pamper the child inside**-it may be as easy as lying in the grass. It may seem silly at first, but don't let others decide your life. Feel the leaves, the breeze, and the sun on your skin. It always brings me back to that moment and gives me a mysterious, childlike feeling that lasts all day.

- **Decide to go slow-**it is the nature that connects us again with the eternity of the moment. At each moment of this consciousness, we return to the title of the world phenomenon of Eckertall, "Power of Now." Torre wakes up his readers for a self-centered life as the creator of suffering and encourages them to live a painless life by living fully in the present. This book is highly recommended for anyone interested in learning the behavior of naturally lean women through the power of mindfulness.

TOOLS FOR INTERRUPTING OBSESSIVE DIETARY THOUGHTS

If you eat too much, you need to develop equality that raises the question of starvation. Step 1 of the Thin Cognitive Behavior protocol is to identify hunger in the brain. If you admit that your hunger is not physical, then step 2 of the protocol is to stop thinking about compulsive diets. Without disturbing the pattern, the obsession with brain hunger becomes stronger when it manifests itself in physiological symptoms. We compared the ability to break obsessive patterns with the mechanism of shifting gears. This is called the caudate of the brain, and if it appears to be stuck, it must be moved manually.

We believe, to some extent, overeating makes us happy and feels good. It's the opposite; they feel embarrassed after most women overeat. By interrupting the pattern, we stop the growth of food thinking strength and begin moving brain hunger out of the compulsion spectrum. Two techniques that we consider to be accessible and effective to prevent obsession with food Eye Movement Desensitization and Reprocessing (EMDR) and emotional freedom techniques (EFT). Both techniques are equally effective in stopping food obsession before a compulsive diet.

- **EDMR- EYE MOVEMENT DESENSITIZATION AND REPROCESSING**

  The EMDR explains that our eye movements are inextricably linked to brain processes. Remembering how delicious this la-carte cake was, your eyes will automatically look up to the left. Given how good it tastes, we look down and look down on the right side. The image below shows how your eyes move to the left when you remember the food, and to the right when you fancy food. The eyes move up, sideways, or down, depending on whether you are fantasizing, listening, or remembering.

The importance of EMDR to our toolbox is that if you're daydreaming about food (looking down from the bottom to the right), you can quickly interrupt your pattern in all directions until your desires stop. EMDR is a simple, light, and effective tool that requires focused eye movements within 30 seconds to keep the brain from sticking to food. This interruption mechanism allows us to stop the typical abduction that occurs when the attraction of food imagination attracts us.

- **EFT- EMOTIONAL FREEDOM TECHNIQUE**

Emotional Freedom Technique (EFT) is another tool that is useful when a pattern break. The acupuncture points used in EFT are listed below and were identified as the end of the meridian in the body centuries before China. When pressure is applied to these points, we shift the energy in our bodies. The EFT process quickly opens these acupoints until the emotional energy changes.

First, ask yourself on a scale of 1-10. One is none; ten is overwhelming how strongly you experience emotional hunger. Let's say you are ten years old. Repeat the following setup statement three times while tapping the left-hand karate intersection. I'm overwhelmingly emotionally hungry, but I accept myself deeply and completely. EFT only works if you believe the setup instructions. If you say the statement out loud and you feel it is not true, you need to modify the statement to fit your beliefs. For example, you can change the setup statement as follows: I'm overwhelmingly emotionally hungry, but I think practicing can change the auto attendant. Focus on your feelings and accept them sincerely. Complete the knock sequence, take a deep breath, and ask yourself.

Has your emotional hunger subsided? If you're still feeling emotional hunger, go back and update your writing to your current level of obsession. For example, if it changes from overwhelming to moderate, change the statement to

Repeat the beating process until emotional hunger is gone. EFT alone does not restore the neural network, but it helps to escape the obsessive-compulsive illusion that fuels overeating. EFT does not restore the NATURALLY THIN WOMEN'S neural network, but staying within the metaphor keeps the car away from the hills, which are more likely to prevent damage.

Following are the acupressure points which work for interruption of food obsession:

1. The inner side of eyebrow near the nose
2. Karate chop
3. Side of eye
4. Collar bone
5. Under the nose
6. On the chin
7. Crown of the head

8. Under the eye – on the cheekbone

- **NLP-NEURO-LINGUISTIC PROGRAMMING**

Anchors are the mental connection between stimulation and reaction. When the stimulus occurs, the reaction from the subconscious mind is automatically invoked. The brain has several anchors. For example, if you experience certain emotions while listening to a song, listening to the same song again will automatically revert those emotions. The advertising industry often uses anchors by creating incentives in food commercials that trigger contextual starvation reactions.

You can develop your anchor by consistently linking selected stimuli to specific emotions. Pressure points are usually set as anchors somewhere on the body. Anchors are compressed when they experience an unwanted sensation. Let's say you want to return to your peace of mind each time you press your left middle finger. Each time you experience peace of mind, you make an anchor by pressing your left middle finger until it becomes an anchor. When the anchor is firmly fixed, and you return to the tornado, press your left middle finger to return to your eyes. A possible scenario would be: You have a very stressful working day. There is no evidence of physical hunger, but it is currently wired to produce stress hormones in difficult, demanding, or hyperbaric situations. Your stress reaction is the feeling of overwhelming emotional hunger that takes you directly to the machine. If you hold your left middle finger at this point, you can feel peace of mind. Inner peace and overeating are mutually exclusive.

So resting and regaining balance can handle anything that needs attention. Anchoring is an effective tool to stop the unconscious and automatic hyperphagic response to many of the triggers that currently govern our behavior.

Many products try to serve the same purpose. They can serve as a springboard for greater progress. However, these products should be used as tools or auxiliary wheels. When these tools are used beyond their intended purpose, NATURALLY THIN WOMEN'S neural network restoration is not supported. If you need a product to get started, you can use it. Keep in mind that auxiliary wheels need to come off at some point so that everyone can learn how to ride a bike.

TOOLS FOR IDENTIFYING ACTUAL NEEDS AND RESPONDING TO WHAT NEEDS ATTENTION

Step 3 consists of two parts. Part 1 is the ability to identify needs that manifest as hunger in the brain. There are many causes for non-physical hunger: social situations (social hunger) that you think you need to eat to adapt, or if you feel socially uncomfortable and believe that overeating makes you feel good. If this can also be caused by an emotional imbalance (emotional hunger), we can't name it, deal with it, or develop it to calm ourselves. As your mindfulness develops, you will have more time to succumb to brain hunger as you better understand the causes of your brain cravings and take on the personal need for self-advocacy. Until the day overeating is history.

Part 2 of Step 3 is a feature that addresses all the needs of hunger. Once you have identified what needs your attention, you can develop skills that meet your needs rather than curb your needs. If we eat or eat too much, we continue the cycle of shame. By having the courage to name and address the underlying needs, we are strengthening a healthy neural network. So, most of it starts with emotions. Following are ways to recognize some of the emotions:

- **Blues**

Low energy with no signs of physical hunger. In most cases, your dopamine levels are low. Moderately intense physical routine and / or meditation can increase dopamine levels to a considerable limit. In chapter 19 of this book, meditation practice with a helpful suggestion is explained.

- **Boring**

Remember that boredom is a form of self-rejection. It's important to work on one of your dream projects, the diary, the vision board, reconnect, and re-invest in one of your life's challenges. If you don't know what your interest is, promise to discover it from now on. There are thousands of resources and workbooks to help you with this search. Shift your energy towards this discovery process. This will take your attention and interest away from thoughts of food.

- **Disappointed**

Express your disappointment clearly and loudly! Call friends, diary, scream! You do not need to stuff yourself with negative thoughts. You should share your insecurities and disappointments with the relevant people.

Otherwise, they will lead to emotional imbalance and eventually to overeating.

• Tired

If you overeat due to chronic sleep deprivation, investing in sleep hygiene best helps your ability to rewire your brain. Meditation is the number one recommendation for improving sleep quality as it calms the monkey. Start the "shutdown cycle" one hour before going to bed. Soothing music, low testosterone levels movies, soothing baths, sensual pajamas, dim light, no computer time, fewer excitement books, in short, a loss that increases the excitement.

• Loneliness

If you are feeling lonely, you may call a friend. Go outside, meet someone. Do something good to someone, even strangers. Go to the hospice or children's crisis management center to help. The urge for food will subside, as the actual problem is mitigated.

- **Anger**

If the problem is chronic, seek treatment from a specialist with anger expertise. If you are occasionally angry, make a loud voice, hit your bag, or walk while expressing anger. You may try to calm yourself by doing meditation or sleeping for some time.

- **Stress Accumulated**

Work out or perform intense exercise. - Scaling down to get the point of view, you have two options: indulge in worst-case thoughts (and increase stress and anxiety) or have the option to let go of your black and white thoughts. Observe meditation for the relief of stress.

- **Lost Control**

Face your worst fear of what loss of control means to you in a general sense. -Are you likely to concentrate on the worst scenario, the black and white way of thinking? -Do you need control? -What are you afraid of failing if you have no control?

If you don't know what you are doing, do a breathing exercise, reconnect to your body, and continue to ask quietly. What do I feel? What is my energy level? "Important changes are exercise, meditation, using your favorite music, keeping a diary of your emotions, or taking a cold shower. It's something you can do immediately rather than unknowingly eat, and that's not a problem as long as you know it helps you pay attention to your real needs. Be prepared to repeat as many times as you need. If, for some reason, you're limited and can't perform an alternate activity, imagine doing it carefully and in stages.

CHAPTER 17: SLEEP LEARNING SYSTEM

Reprogramming the subconscious mind during sleep is a very effective method that can be used to make positive changes in our lives and reveal goals. There are various tools you can use to get some sleep time.

As we grow older, it makes sense that our lives get busier. Many people recognize that the mind is as important as the rest of us, and that programming it well is also important.

How can we change, how we see things, our feelings for a particular idea, and how we carry ourselves? It is only natural that our subconsciousness is a powerful force in us because we all have a subconscious mind that remembers everything and preserves our beliefs and feelings. It acquires a specific pattern at a very young age and consequently forms most of the habits that we do most of the time unconsciously.

Many people may want to change some part of their lives, but they don't necessarily want to use their work or effort, but others don't know where to start. The truth is that you have to reprogram your subconscious to see the change. One way to do this is to reprogram the subconscious during sleep. Since we live a hustle life, it's much more effective to do this when we're asleep than when we're awake, because it's easy to be distracting.

Few people know that the subconscious never sleeps or stops. It always works, paying attention to and taking in everything that is happening, even when we are asleep. You can reprogram virtually anything by yourself. Some things you can improve with sleep include improving self-confidence, improving relationships, learning to love yourself, and promoting a business career.

Overall, reprogramming the subconscious requires replacing old restrictive beliefs and bad habits with new positive beliefs. Our subconscious is programmed between 1 and 7 years.

This means that many of us have retained our unhelpful negative beliefs and bad habits since we were young. In these times, our beliefs depend heavily on our parents, the way we set up our homes, and the people around us. As we grow older, we discover more and more to become better people and reach our goals. It's harder to move forward if we still have past threads to solve now because we have different ages, different mindsets, different lifestyles.

Now that we know how important it is to reprogram the subconscious, an effective way to do this during sleep is to speak to yourself using assertions. Before going to bed at night, you need to be positive and strong about what you are working on and what you want to do to change your life.

Confirmation is more powerful when expressed in the present as if they were already true. Do not use future assertions as if they happened or should have happened. For example, if your goal is to build muscle and your body has recently become non-muscle, this is "I'm healthy and strong, I have big muscles throughout my body, and It's a strong and positive affirmation like "I like the feel," as strong an affirmation of the nation. If you listen to yourself with a positive and strong assertion before going to bed each night, you are more likely to dream of how to reach your goals. This is one of the ways our subconscious mind speaks to us.

The University of San Diego has proven that reprogramming the subconscious mind during sleep is more effective than hypnosis. Many recruits use this technique to assist in training. A very powerful technique is to say yes at bedtime. My eyes begin to close, and I feel sleepy. Immediately before going to sleep, you are in a theta mental state, where suggestions and confirmations easily occur unknowingly. Imagine what you could do with it every night before bed!

The second way to reprogram the subconscious mind during sleep is to hear a positive stimulating voice. You can use the pre-recorded audio that you have verified, or you can create your own audio. Share your affirmation with your recording device and play it automatically overnight. In addition to affirmations, you can record and tell the specific scene you want and hear it during your sleep. You can do this while sleeping or before bed, as your subconscious mind is awake and recording everything.

The subconscious mind is always functional, so listening to audio while sleeping is the same as listening to it while you are awake. Many think that they can't remember or hear, but the subconscious has already learned and heard, whether or not they are conscious. The next day you feel more vibrant, positive, and open, and suddenly you are full of ideas. This is evidence that the subconscious has absorbed audio information during rest.

The subconscious mind controls about 90-95% of our actions. This proves to us that our subconscious mind is ours today and plays a major role in the way we present ourselves to the world. The sooner you realize that the mind is as important as our body, the more you can rule your life and prevent it from controlling you.

CHAPTER 18: WEIGHT LOSS AFFIRMATIONS

In this chapter, we will learn about weight loss affirmations. Weight loss affirmations are a great way to stimulate your journey to weight loss. You can use these positive weight loss affirmations to program your mind with positive habits.

We all know that weight loss is not easy. The use of these weight loss affirmations can help people facing stubborn internal resistance when trying to lose weight.

These are the affirmations that you can suggest yourself while practicing self-hypnosis, cognitive-behavioral theory, or Sleep learning system. In the first two methods, these affirmations can directly be suggested, and in the third method, you can record these and listen to them while sleeping.

You must be careful while choosing theses affirmations. It is suggested that you should select the affirmations that you believe yourself and do not raise an objection when they are suggested to you. The failure happens because if you do not believe yourself, then it will not work for you. Moreover, it is suggested that you use a few affirmations that you think are effective for you. Do not try to suggest all at once. It may retard the effectiveness of the methods. There are also chances that the brain may become confused in case of any two opposite affirmations. So, better select your affirmations very carefully.

Now we will list the affirmations for excessive weight loss:

• Weight loss makes sense to me.

• I want to reach the goal of weight loss.

• I lose weight every day.

• I love to exercise regularly.

• I eat foods that contribute to my health and well-being.

• I only eat when I am hungry.

• I can see myself clearly with my ideal weight.

• I love the taste of healthy food.

- I can control how much I want to eat.

- I like training. I feel better.

- Through exercise, I will be stronger and stronger every day.

- I can reach the ideal weight and maintain it.

- I love and care for my body.

- I deserve a slim, healthy, and attractive body.

- I always have a healthier eating habit.

- I lose weight every day.

- It looks good and feels good.

- I can do what it takes to be healthy.

- I am happy to redefine success.

- I decided to train.

- I want to eat food that looks and feels good.

- I am responsible for my health.

- I love my body.

- I put up with building a better body for myself.

- When I wake up, I have a great time doing exercise every morning to achieve my desired weight loss.

- I am working on a weight loss program by changing my diet from unhealthy to healthy.

- I am happy with everything I do to lose weight.

- I get thinner and healthier every day.

- I am developing an attractive body.

- I develop a lifestyle with life health.

- I can create a body that I will like and enjoy.

These were general affirmations that you can use in a normal condition. You can move to more specific affirmations later, when you feel that now it is time to modify my practice. Some of these affirmations are given below that will help you cope up with weight gain with a more specific approach.

• Discovering my unique diet and exercise system for weight loss is exciting.

• I accept and enjoy my sexuality. You can feel it sensually.

• I am a beautiful person.

• I am a lovable person. I deserve love. It is safe for me to lose weight.

• I am a weight loss success story.

• I am happy to lose 20 pounds.

• I am ready to develop new ideas about myself and my body.

• I choose to trust the ability to make positive changes in my life.

- I congratulate myself on choosing the right food.

- I drink eight glasses of water daily.

- I eat fruits and vegetables every day, mainly chicken and fish.

- I enjoy walking 3-4 times a week and have at least three toning exercised a week.

- I free the need to criticize my body.

- I have a strong weight in the world due to my low weight.

- I learn and use mental, emotional, and spiritual skills for success. Ready to change!

- I love and appreciate my body.

- I will take care of my body in optimal health.

- I'm happy that I have the ideal weight.

- It feels good to move your body. The practice is fun!

• It feels great to have lost more than £ 10 in 4 weeks and can't wait to meet my girlfriend.

• It's easy to follow a healthy diet plan.

• My lifestyle changes my body.

• My metabolism is excellent.

• My stomach is flat.

• Take a deep breath to relax and deal with stress.

• My efforts are worth reaching the ideal weight.

You can make your own affirmation to that suit your routine and efforts. These affirmations in a normal routine or combined with methods that we discussed in this e-book can help reduce the weight quickly without affecting the emotional health.

CHAPTER 19: MEDITATION FOR WEIGHT LOSS

Meditation is a daily exercise, where you clear your mind and return to a place of calm thought and emotion. Some people only practice 5 minutes a day, but most meditation specialists recommend working up to 20 minutes a day.

Meditation is not difficult. If you're just getting started, immediately wake up and spend 5 minutes to cleanse your mind before a busy day. Close your eyes and concentrate without trying to change your breathing pattern. Just focus on your breathing. If your mind wanders and it's probably the first-just put it back into your breath without judgment.

Libshtein recommends practice 10 minutes a day (5 minutes in the morning, 5 minutes in the evening) but finds that "time is not as important as just doing it regularly." Developing new habits can be difficult. So, if you start with 5 minutes a day, that's fine. If you find it most comfortable for you, feel free to sit and lie down.

"Meditation is an effective way to help people lose weight," Libshtein says. What made meditation so powerful in this regard? "Agreeing to the changes we want to apply to our behavior reconciles consciousness and unconsciousness," he explains. These changes include controlling cravings for unhealthy foods and changing diets. It is important to include the subconscious. The reason is that the harmful and weight gaining behaviors, such as emotional eating, are fixed. Meditation can help to recognize it and nullify it in some exercises, and even replace it with a slimming habit.

But meditation will soon pay off. "Meditation can directly reduce stress hormone levels," explains Libshtein. Stress hormones such as cortisol signal our bodies to store calories as fat. If large amounts of cortisol are pumped through your system, it will be difficult to lose even if you make a healthy decision. That seems difficult. We are all stressed, and it seems impossible to shake. However, a study by Carnegie Mellon University found that 25 minutes of meditation for three consecutive days was required to significantly reduce stress.

According to Yi-Yuan Tang, the chair of the neuroscience funded by the president and a professor of psychology at the Texas Institute of Technology. Research shows that self-control may also increase with daily practice. Researchers have found that the parts of the brain most affected by meditation help control ourselves. So, by meditating for a few minutes a day, you can easily pass this second cookie and avoid ice if you feel unwell.

How can meditation help you when dieting and exercising go wrong?

"Stress is often the main cause of excessive weight gain or inability to lose weight effectively," explains Libstein. So, if you're on a diet or exercise and you're constantly stressed, you may not be solving your weight problems. Again, stress releases hormones that store additional fat; that's exactly the thing we don't want! It can also trigger a stress cycle. You cannot lose weight because you are under stress, and you feel stress because you cannot lose weight. It's an easy pattern to get stuck, but you can break it-and meditation can help.

To successfully manage or relieve stress, you first need to understand what causes most of your stress in life. Some stressors are easy to identify, while others are subtle. "I recommend using WellBe to understand, monitor, and address stress," says Libshtein. The WellBe is a bracelet that acts as a physical activity tracker but is the first of its kind to focus on emotional well-being instead.

If you want to add meditation to your weight loss weapon, it's important not to stress it. Meditation is designed to help relieve stress and does not cause stress. For this reason, we asked Libhstein for three easy ways to incorporate calm habits into our daily lives without feeling this is an additional obligation or task. Of course, practicing meditation and spending a few minutes each day will give you the best results.

You can create a mantra to focus on your goals. A mantra is a word or phrase that focuses on your practice and repeats to bring you back to the center when you are wandering. As Libshtein explains, "Mantras can give you something to focus on during meditation." Many find it useful in practice, but especially what you appeal to. If you choose, it is not necessary. If it feels natural or useless, you don't have to force yourself to use it. If you choose either, Libshtein recommends repeating as you inhale and exhale. Common choices are "I am loved," "I am peaceful," and "Om." If the mantra doesn't feel right to you, Libshtein tells you to focus on your breathing.

"Try to use four counts for inhalation and eight counts for exhalation," Libshtein suggests. But meditation is to reduce stress. If these counts feel tense or unnatural, you can deviate from them. Try increasing the number each time you meditate. "Don't worry if you need time to perform up to eight counts," says Libshtein. "We only know that stretching your breath can calm you down considerably."

There are many records, podcasts, websites, and phone apps that connect you to an expert who can guide you in meditation exercises until you feel alone. The Libshtein website, Mentors Channel, is just one example of such a service.

Look for guided meditations that focus on it, especially if you want to use meditation for weight loss. Video or audio recording professionals will ask you to imagine various things: how they look and feel after losing weight, the moving person who has already lost weight, and what they can think and feel? What they are likely to do to succeed in losing weight and losing weight, and how these habits can be integrated into their daily lives.

Meditation is just one of the entire weight loss toolkits. Diet and exercise are also important parts of the equation, and combining all three to create a long-lasting lifestyle always yields the best results. The key to meditation, such as eating and exercising, is dedication. You need to stick to practice to witness the permanent changes. "Research shows that meditation alters the structure of the brain after long practice, for example immediately after 21 days," says Libshtein. That's why the Mentors Channel offers a 21-day program. This program allows you to see permanent changes.

Preparing for success will make it easier for you to begin your meditation routine. Creating a calm meditation room, including meditation equipment, can facilitate your practice.

CHAPTER 20: FORBIDDEN FOODS

One of the main mistakes in weight loss strategies is to avoid or minimize the entire food category (fat, carbohydrates, sugar, etc.). Finally, what we understand is that classifying foods as forbidden, instigates the brain to an obsession with more of such foods. We now understand that withdrawing all categories of food to establish healthy eating behavior is counterproductive. The reason is simple. As long as we believe these foods are "banned," they retain high emotional values for us, as well as the power of illegal love arouses to crave such foods even more.

Marking these foods as banned is harmful as it creates an effect called the Polar bear effect, and the person cannot resist always thinking about the forbidden food items. Humans crave something prohibited, for it is a part of human nature. Researchers call this the "forbidden fruit hypothesis." At the moment we experience the exhaustion of our ego, we encounter these uncontrollable "forbidden fruit hypothesis" when there are difficult days when we need to feel at ease and comfort like a moth of light. This feeling explains the frenzy and frustration when we eat these foods after the suppression mechanism is exhausted.

Cognitive studies have shown that exposure to food triggers and prevention of reactions is a very effective technique for rewiring the brain. If you learn to not force yourself to eat, you must reintroduce "Forbidden Foods" and eliminate the illusion of food.

When we can trust that we can eat with all our hearts, eating what we want is paramount. Then miracles will occur! We choose to eat nutritious, cheerful foods, and when we eat "forbidden foods," we do not overeat them anymore. Therefore, the solution is to use the TCB protocol to control mindful eating. If you have the evidence that your mindfulness connections are well-developed and you can be convinced that you can eat those foods in a normal limit. Even if they are initially mechanistic, until these fascinating powers disappear, it is important to include prohibited foods in your menu.

A person banned having nachos and ice cream at home while he had a pointless meal. But after a particularly rewarding day in the office, he usually stopped by a supermarket and, as you might imagine, bought a bag of nacho chips and some ice cream tubs. Then he overdosed these forbidden foods. The moment the attack ended, he hit himself. The next day, he gave his friend the rest of the ice cream and nacho chips. This act is a performance that has been repeated over and over again in his life.

After understanding the effects of ego depletion concerning the forbidden fruit hypothesis, his story of oppression, and finally biting makes sense. Next, his goal was to plan a meal with Nachos as the main event. He made a nacho supreme, ordered a nacho platter at a restaurant, and devised my own nachos recipe with healthy toppings. A week after the Nacho Festival, the bag of tortilla chips was able to stand in the kitchen without fear or difficulty. The forbidden food technique is out of date and must be discarded now. You have now mysterious power up your sleeves.

Whenever we see a naturally thin woman claiming that she can eat whatever she wants, we think that how is that even possible. The answer is, although they do not ban food for them, but they do not overeat them. Their mind produces enough dopamine with minor amounts of such foods. So, to conclude, we need to know that there is no need for banning food categories anymore. Let not your dopamine level exhaust over such small things. Change your wiring and eat all you want, while staying in control.

Food for all!

CONCLUSION

This book is a blend of all the effective techniques to help people who are suffering from excessive weight gain. It presents a different dimension of how the key to weight loss lies in your brain. It covers the techniques of self-hypnosis, Cognitive behavioral therapy (CBT), Sleep Learning, and Meditation. All of these techniques involve the active involvement of the brain and change in the wiring pattern of the brain to raise a satisfactory level of the brain to stop the urges of overeating. The book contains a detailed account of all the activities, processes, and requirements to make all these techniques work out for you in a healthy manner.

This book serves multiple purposes. It not only guides about weight loss techniques but also the root causes of the other emotional problems that promote overeating. This book serves as a complete guide to a fatless, healthy, happy, and satisfactory lifestyle.

COPYRIGHTS

©Copyright by Karen Loss 2020

All rights reserved

This book: **"RAPID WEIGHT LOSS HYPNOSIS:** Extreme Weight-Loss Hypnosis for Woman! How to Fat Burning & Calorie Blast, Lose Weight with Meditation & Affirmations, Mini Habits, Self-Hypnosis. Stop Emotional Eating!**"**

Written by Karen Loss

This document aims to provide precise and reliable details on this subject and the problem under discussion.

The product is marketed on the assumption that no officially approved bookkeeping or publishing house provides other available funds.

Where a legal or qualified guide is required, a person must have the right to participate in the field.

A statement of principle, which is a subcommittee of the American Bar Association, a committee of publishers and Associations and approved. A copy, reproduction, or distribution of parts of this text, in electronic or written form, is not permitted.

The recording of this Document is strictly prohibited, and any retention of this text is only with the written permission of the publisher and all Liberties authorized.

The information provided here is correct and reliable, as any lack of attention or other means resulting from the misuse or use of the procedures, procedures, or instructions contained therein is the total, and absolute obligation of the user addressed.

The author is not obliged, directly or indirectly, to assume civil or civil liability for any restoration, damage, or loss resulting from the data collected here. The respective authors retain all copyrights not kept by the publisher.

The information contained herein is solely and universally available for information purposes. The data is presented without a warranty or promise of any kind.

The trademarks used are without approval, and the patent is issued without the trademark owner's permission or protection. The logos and labels in this book are the property of the owners themselves and are not associated with this text.

CPSIA information can be obtained
at www.ICGtesting.com
Printed in the USA
LVHW050526231220
674888LV00007B/144